PENPALS *for* Handwriting

Foundation 2 Teacher's Book (4–5 years)

Gill Budgell   Kate Ruttle

Series Consultants
Sue Palmer   Professor Rhona Stainthorp

CW00541067

Contents

CAMBRIDGE   **HITACHI**

www.cambridge-hitachi.com

Foundation 1/3–5 years

DEVELOPING GROSS MOTOR SKILLS
1 The vocabulary of movement
2 Large movements
3 Responding to music

DEVELOPING FINE MOTOR SKILLS
4 Hand and finger play
5 Making and modelling
6 Links to art
7 Using one-handed tools and equipment

DEVELOPING PATTERNS AND BASIC LETTER MOVEMENTS
8 Pattern-making
9 Responding to music
10 Investigating straight line patterns
11 Investigating loops
12 Investigating circles
13 Investigating angled patterns
14 Investigating eights and spirals

Foundation 2/Primary 1

Term 2
1 Introducing long ladder letters: l, i, t, u, j, y
2 Practising long ladder letters: l, i
3 Practising long ladder letters: t, u
4 Practising long ladder letters: j, y
5 Practising all the long ladder letters
6 Introducing one-armed robot letters: r, b, n, h, m, k, p
7 Practising one-armed robot letters: b, n
8 Practising one-armed robot letters: h, m
9 Practising one-armed robot letters: k, p
10 Practising all the one-armed robot letters
11 Introducing capitals for one-armed robot letters: R, B, N, H, M, K, P
12 Introducing capitals for long ladder letters: L, I, T, U, J, Y

Term 3
13 Introducing curly caterpillar letters: c, a, d, o, s, g, q, e, f
14 Practising curly caterpillar letters: a, d
15 Practising curly caterpillar letters: o, s
16 Practising curly caterpillar letters: g, q
17 Practising curly caterpillar letters: e, f
18 Practising all the curly caterpillar letters
19 Introducing zig-zag monster letters: z, v, w, x
20 Practising zig-zag monster letters: v, w, x
21 Introducing capitals for curly caterpillar letters: C, A, D, O, S, G, Q, E, F
22 Introducing capitals for zig-zag monster letters: Z, V, W, X
23 Exploring ch, th and sh

Year 1/Primary 2

Term 1
1 Letter formation practice: long ladder family
2 Letter formation practice: one-armed robot family
3 Letter formation practice: curly caterpillar family
4 Letter formation practice: zig-zag monster family
5 Practising the vowels: i
6 Practising the vowels: u
7 Practising the vowels: a
8 Practising the vowels: o
9 Practising the vowels: e
10 Letter formation practice: capital letters

Term 2
11 Introducing diagonal join to ascender: joining at, all
12 Practising diagonal join to ascender: joining th
13 Practising diagonal join to ascender: joining ch
14 Practising diagonal join to ascender: joining cl
15 Introducing diagonal join, no ascender: joining un, um
16 Practising diagonal join, no ascender: joining cr, tr, dr
17 Practising diagonal join, no ascender: joining lp, mp
18 Introducing diagonal join, no ascender, to an anticlockwise letter:
joining id, ig
19 Practising diagonal join, no ascender, to an anticlockwise letter:
joining nd, ld
20 Practising diagonal join, no ascender, to an anticlockwise letter:
joining ng

Term 3
21 Practising diagonal join, no ascender: joining ee
22 Practising diagonal join, no ascender: joining ai, ay
23 Practising diagonal join, no ascender: joining une, ine
24 Introducing horizontal join, no ascender: joining op, oy
25 Practising horizontal join, no ascender: joining one, ome
26 Introducing horizontal join, no ascender, to an anticlockwise letter:
joining oa, og
27 Practising horizontal join, no ascender, to an anticlockwise letter:
joining wa, wo
28 Introducing horizontal join to ascender: joining ot, ot
29 Practising horizontal join to ascender: joining wh, oh
30 Introducing horizontal and diagonal joins to ascender, to an
anticlockwise letter: joining of, if
31 Assessment

Year 2/Primary 3

Term 1
1 How to join in a word: high-frequency words
2 Introducing the break letters: j, g, x, y, z, b, f, p, q, r, s
3 Practising diagonal join to ascender in words: ed, ect
4 Practising diagonal join, no ascender, in words: a_e
5 Practising diagonal join, no ascender, to an
anticlockwise letter in words: ice, ide
6 Practising diagonal join, no ascender, in words: ow, ou
7 Practising horizontal join, no ascender, in words: oy, oi
8 Practising horizontal join, no ascender, to an
anticlockwise letter in words: oa, ode
9 Practising horizontal join to ascender in words: ole, obe
10 Practising horizontal join to ascender in words: ook, ool

Term 2
11 Practising diagonal join to r: ir, ur, er
12 Practising horizontal join to r: or, oor
13 Introducing horizontal join from r to ascender: urt, irt, irt
14 Introducing horizontal join from r to ascender: ere
15 Practising joining to and from r: air
16 Introducing diagonal join to s: dis
17 Introducing horizontal join to s: ws
18 Introducing diagonal join from s to ascender: sh
19 Introducing diagonal join from s, no ascender: si, su, se, sp, sm
20 Introducing horizontal join from r to an anticlockwise letter: rs

Term 3
21 Practising diagonal join to an anticlockwise letter: ea, ear
22 Introducing horizontal join to and from f to ascender: ft, ff
23 Introducing horizontal join from f to ascender: fu, ff
24 Introducing qu (diagonal join, no ascender)
25 Introducing rr (horizontal join, no ascender)
26 Introducing ss (diagonal join, no ascender, to an anticlockwise letter)
27 Introducing ff (horizontal join to ascender)
28 Capital letter practice: height of ascenders and capitals
29 Assessment
30 Assessment

Scope and sequence

Year 3 / Primary 4

Term 1
1 Revising joins in a word: long vowel phonemes
2 Revising joins in a word: *le*
3 Revising joins in a word: *ing*
4 Revising joins in a word: high-frequency words
5 Revising joins in a word: new vocabulary
6 Revising joins in a word: *un, de*
7 Revising joins to and from s: *dis*
8 Revising joins to and from r: *re, pre*
9 Revising joins to and from f: *ff*
10 Revising joins: *qu*

Term 2
11 Introducing joining b and p: diagonal join, no ascender, *bi, bu, pi, pu*
12 Practising joining b and p: diagonal join, no ascender, to an anticlockwise letter, *ba, bo, pa, po*
13 Practising joining b and p: diagonal join to ascender, *bl, ph*
14 Relative sizes of letters: silent letters
15 Parallel ascenders: high-frequency words
16 Parallel descenders: adding *y* to words
17 Relative size and consistency: *ly, less, ful*
18 Relative size and consistency: capitals
19 Speed and fluency practice: *er, est*
20 Speed and fluency practice: opposites

Term 3
21 Consistency in spacing: *mis, anti, ex*
22 Consistency in spacing: *non, co*
23 Consistency in spacing: apostrophes
24 Layout, speed and fluency practice: address
25 Layout, speed and fluency practice: dialogue
26 Layout, speed and fluency practice: poem
27 Layout, speed and fluency practice: letter
28 Handwriting style
29 Assessment
30 Handwriting style

Year 4 / Primary 5

Term 1
1 Revising joins in a word: *ness, ship*
2 Revising joins in a word: *ing, ed*
3 Revising joins in a word: *s*
4 Revising joins in a word: *ify*
5 Revising joins in a word: *nn, mm, ss*
6 Revising parallel ascenders: *tt, ll, bb*
7 Revising parallel ascenders and descenders: *pp, ff*
8 Revising joins to an anticlockwise letter: *cc, dd*
9 Revising break letters: alphabetical order
10 Linking spelling and handwriting: related words

Term 2
11 Introducing sloped writing
12 Parallel ascenders: *al, ad, af*
13 Parallel descenders and break letters: *ight, ough*
14 Size, proportion and spacing: *ious*
15 Size, proportion and spacing: *able, ful*
16 Size, proportion and spacing: *fs, ves*
17 Speed and fluency: abbreviations for notes
18 Speed and fluency: notemaking
19 Speed and fluency: drafting
20 Speed and fluency: lists

Term 3
21 Size, proportion and spacing: *v, k*
22 Size, proportion and spacing: *ic, ist*
23 Size, proportion and spacing: *ion*
24 Size, proportion and spacing: contractions
25 Speed and fluency: *ible, able*
26 Speed and fluency: diminutives
27 Print alphabet
28 Print capitals
29 Assessment
30 Presentational skills: font styles

Years 5 & 6 / Primary 6 & 7

Year 5 Handwriting
1 Revision: practising sloped writing
2 Revision: practising the joins
3 Developing style for speed: joining from *t*
4 Developing style for speed: looping from *g, j* and *y*
5 Developing style for speed: joining from *f*
6 Developing style for speed: joining from *s*
7 Developing style for speed: writing *v, w, x* and *z* at speed
8 Developing style for speed: pen breaks in longer words
9 Different styles for different purposes
10 Assessment

Year 5 Project work
11 Haiku project: making notes
12 Haiku project: organising ideas
13 Haiku project: producing a draft
14 Haiku project: publishing the haiku
15 Haiku project: evaluation
16 Letter project: making notes
17 Letter project: structuring an argument
18 Letter project: producing a draft
19 Letter project: publishing a letter
20 Letter project: evaluation

Year 6 Handwriting
21 Self-assessment: evaluating handwriting
22 Self-assessment: checking the joins
23 Self-assessment: consistency of size
24 Self-assessment: letters resting on baseline
25 Self-assessment: ascenders and descenders
26 Self-assessment: consistency of size of capitals and ascenders
27 Writing at speed: inappropriate closing of letters
28 Writing at speed: identifying unclosed letters
29 Writing at speed: spacing within words
30 Writing at speed: spacing between words

Year 6 Project work
31 Playscript project: collecting information
32 Playscript project: recording ideas
33 Playscript project: producing a draft
34 Playscript project: publishing a playscript
35 Playscript project: evaluation
36 Information notice project: collecting and organising information
37 Information notice project: organising information
38 Information notice project: producing a draft
39 Information notice project: publishing a notice
40 Information notice project: evaluation

Penpals rationale

Even in this computer-literate age, good handwriting remains fundamental to our children's educational achievement. *Penpals for Handwriting* will help you teach children to develop fast, fluent, legible handwriting. This carefully structured handwriting scheme can also make a difference to overall attainment in writing.

Traditional principles in the contemporary classroom

We believe that:

1 A flexible, fluent and legible handwriting style empowers children to write with confidence and creativity. This is an entitlement that needs skilful teaching if each individual is to reach their full potential at primary school.

2 Handwriting is a developmental process with its own distinctive stages of sequential growth. We have identified five stages that form the basic organisational structure of *Penpals*:
   1 Readiness for handwriting; gross and fine motor skills; pattern and letter formation (Foundation / 3–5 years)
   2 Beginning to join (Key Stage 1 / 5–7 years)
   3 Securing the joins (Key Stage 1 and lower Key Stage 2 / 5–9 years)
   4 Practising speed and fluency (lower Key Stage 2 / 7–9 years)
   5 Presentation skills (upper Key Stage 2 / 9–11 years)

3 Handwriting must be actively taught: this can be done in association with spelling. Learning to associate the kinaesthetic handwriting movement with the visual letter pattern and the aural phonemes will help children learn to spell.

Through the supportive context of whole-class activities leading to independent tasks, *Penpals* develops:

● control of fine and gross movements that support the development of handwriting;
● vocabulary for talking about letter formation;
● oral patter to support the formation of letters within their letter families;
● links between phonemes and letters;
● efficient pencil hold and good posture;
● control of pencil marks to form letters correctly, to prepare for joining;
● opportunities for exploring shape and movement across the curriculum and in the environment.

A practical approach

Penpals offers a practical approach to support the delivery of handwriting teaching in the context of the modern curriculum:

● **Time** *Penpals'* focus on whole-class teaching, with key teaching points clearly identified, allows effective teaching in the time available.
● **Planning** *Penpals* helps with long-, medium- and short-term planning for each key stage correlated to national guidelines.
● **Practice** *Penpals* offers pupil Practice Books with their own internal structure of excellent models for finger tracing, pencil tracing and independent writing.
● **Revision** *Penpals* offers opportunities for record-keeping, review and assessment throughout the course.
● **Motivation** The *Penpals* materials are attractive and well-designed with the support of handwriting experts to stimulate and motivate children.
● **ICT** Use the *Penpals* CD-ROMs to enrich and extend children's handwriting experiences.

A few words from the experts...

Sue Palmer *literacy specialist and educational writer*

Handwriting has often been the 'Cinderella-skill' in terms of the teaching of writing and too many published resources have relied far too much (and too soon) on worksheet materials. For many young children, worksheets in Nursery and Reception classes can often be counterproductive. Instead, we should be linking preparation for handwriting to music, movement and art, and ensuring that these experiences are both appropriate for handwriting and enjoyable for the children. In this respect, the practical suggestions in *Penpals* are the best materials I have ever come across.

Catherine Elsey *State Registered Occupational Therapist, National Handwriting Association*

Handwriting is the ultimate fine motor task, which additionally requires skills in eye–hand co-ordination, organisation and sequencing. We expect these skills of very young children, all too often before they are developmentally ready, for example requiring fine motor control of fingers before having postural stability. Pre-writing skills can be learnt by young children, but we should not expect letter and number formation until they can master an oblique cross (X), which requires crossing midline. Children with illegible handwriting or where writing causes discomfort have often picked up 'bad habits' when younger. Many children with handwriting difficulties are referred to Occupational Therapists who can help improve letter formation, fluency and pencil grip for example, but it would be of greater benefit to make sure children get the basics of handwriting correct at the outset. *Penpals for Handwriting* will help establish the right skills at the right time for each child and so make this essential communication tool a pleasure rather than a chore.

Links to national guidelines

Penpals Foundation 2 supports many national guidelines including:

- *Early Years Foundation Stage* (EYFS);
- *Primary Frameworks for literacy and mathematics* (Primary National Strategy 2006);
- *Letters and sounds – Principles and Practice of High Quality Phonics* (DfES 2007);
- *Curriculum Framework for Children 3 to 5* (Scottish Consultative Council on the Curriculum);
- *The Northern Ireland Curriculum: Primary* (CCEA).

Penpals and phonics

Penpals gives children the opportunity to revisit and consolidate their growing knowledge of phonics and spelling while securing the kinaesthetic movements needed for a legible, fast and fluent handwriting style.

It is envisaged that *Penpals* Foundation 1 and Foundation 2 will be used throughout the Foundation stage and alongside the chosen resource for delivering the discrete daily phonics session.

Penpals Foundation 1 is ideally suited to children working within Phases 1 and 2 of *Letters and Sounds*, while Foundation 2 goes on to cover Phases 3 and 4.

In the *Penpals* Foundation 2, Year 1 and Year 2 CD-ROMs the word banks give opportunities for learning handwriting in the context of words that are easy to read and spell. After each handwriting movement has been introduced and practised it is recommended that you revise the movement with a phonics focus in line with the appropriate *Letters and sounds* phase.

By Year 3 the transition from phonics into spelling has been made. All of the screens in the *Penpals* Year 3, Year 4 and Years 5 & 6 CD-ROMs create opportunities to revisit and secure spelling patterns while developing a confident and fluent handwriting style.

This chart links the units in the *Penpals* Foundation 2 CD-ROM with additional phonics practice. Also included in this chart are some high-frequency words that will be useful for practising spelling and for developing handwriting.

Year	Letters and sounds phase	Penpals F2 CD-ROM unit	Phonic words including high-frequency decodable words	High-frequency tricky and decodable words for additional practice
Reception	3	5 l, i, t, u, j, y	lit, till, tut, Jill, it	I
	3	10 r, b, n, h, m k, p	my, but, hill, run, up, rub, in, mum	him, put
	4	18 c, a, d, o, s, g, q, e, f	quack, mess, egg, off, kick, rain, feet, night, boat, boot	to, you, all, go, no, are, be, me, said
	4	20 z, v, w, x	cow, fox, van, zip, buzz, next, swim, switch, went, when	was, have, were, what, we
	4	23 sh, ch, th	shop, thing, thin, with, moth, much, crash, shark, splash, chimps	the, they, she, this, that, them

Classroom organisation

The ideal classroom organisation for teaching *Penpals* is to have the children sitting at desks or tables arranged so that they can all see the interactive white board (IWB). Each child needs a dry-wipe board (preferably with guidelines) and a marker pen, or pencil and paper.

If this organisation is not possible within your classroom, bear in mind the following points as you plan your own classroom:

- All the children need to see the IWB and be able to copy words or handwriting patterns from it. (Copying may not be appropriate for children in the earlier stages.)
- Handwriting is usually done on a horizontal or slightly sloped surface.

When to use *Penpals*

Penpals can be used flexibly to teach handwriting. Ideally the whole-class teaching session will be followed immediately by the independent work, but where this is not possible the sessions may be split.

Timing the sessions

The whole-class session for each unit, including the warm-up activities, should take no more than 15 minutes. The independent working session should take about 15–20 minutes.

In addition to the allocated time, extra daily 'practice times' of 5–10 minutes are ideal, if the practicalities of your timetable allow for it. Children can use these sessions to practise the high-frequency words, to extend their pattern practice or to revisit the letter pattern shown in the Practice Books. As with most successful learning, 'little and often' is the most effective approach.

Gross and fine motor skills

In *Penpals: Foundation 1*, a series of units based upon developing gross motor skills, fine motor skills and basic letter movements is offered as a resource base. These will need to be taught and revisited at several stages throughout the Foundation phase. The shape of the *Foundation 2* lessons is generally assumed to be that of moving from gross to fine motor skills.

Teaching units

In *Penpals: Foundation 2*, 23 teaching units are provided for terms 2 and 3 (by which time most of the intake are in school). In subsequent years, 10 units have been provided for each school term.

Teaching sequence for a unit of *Penpals for Handwriting*

You will need:

- the Foundation 2 CD-ROM;
- the relevant Teacher's Book page;
- the Big Book and water-based marker pens.

Children will need:

- space for sky writing and movement;
- dry-wipe boards and marker pens* or pencils and paper;
- pencils and coloured pencils;
- the relevant Practice Book.

(*Remember that one of the crucial elements of ensuring good handwriting is good posture. If children are writing with dry-wipe boards on their knees or on the floor, good posture is more difficult to achieve.)

Whole-class session

The *Foundation 2 CD-ROM* can be used for whole-class teaching.

Warm-up clips Gross and fine motor control activities are accessible from the main menu of the CD-ROM. Use these at the start of each lesson to ensure that children's body and fingers are prepared.

1   **Unit focus and phonic links** These are clearly identified for each unit.

2   **Units** Every unit begins with a whole-class teaching session based on the CD-ROM and usually includes a focus letter animation, a challenge artwork, a word bank and a skywriting animation.

4   **Letter animation** These activities provide opportunities to demonstrate and talk about correct letter formation. Children can practise tracing and copying the letters. Children also benefit from additional skywriting practice, tracing the handwriting pattern on their palms, on each other's back, on the table in front of them, etc.

5   **Challenge artwork** These pictures represent a word beginning with the target letter. Children identify the word, write it and establish the target letter.

3   **Sky writing** These activities involve children drawing patterns in the air. They are an ideal way of introducing a gross motor movement before refining it as a fine motor movement.

6   **Word bank** These activities provide banks of differentiated words that you can use to model and discuss letter formation and phonemes. Children can practise tracing the target graphemes in words.

9   **Gross and fine motor skills** Additional activities (often linked to ideas from *Penpals Foundation 1* Teacher's Book) for developing these essential skills.

8   **Play and practise** Pattern practice for any medium is suggested for children who are not ready to put pen to paper in the Practice Books.

7   **Show alphabet** (F1–Y4) Animations showing how to form all capital and lower case letters.

Independent work

This session can follow on directly from the whole-class session. Ideally, the children's work should be overseen by an adult. Part 2 of the teacher's notes for each unit provides helpful advice on using the pupil's Practice Book page together and highlights some common errors to avoid.

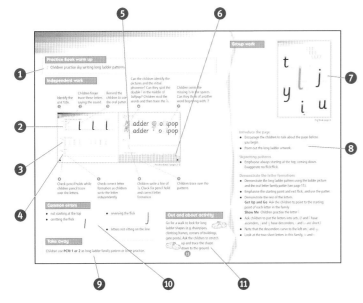

In Foundation 2/P1, children record their work in write-in Practice Books (for terms 2 and 3). They should have a sharpened pencil for their writing, but may also need coloured pencils for pattern practice.

1 Practice Book warm up An optional warm up for use where there is a split between the whole-class session and the independent work.

The left-hand page of the Practice Book (with starting dot support)

2 Finger tracing The unit which introduces each letter family always begins with finger-tracing letters that incorporate the representative artwork (e.g. curly caterpillar, long ladder).

3 Pencil tracing with starting dots to support letter formation.

4 Independent writing with an initial pencil trace and dots to indicate the correct starting point.

The right-hand page of the Practice Book

5 Copying letters in context Once the children have practised forming the letters, they should try to write them in a context (usually a simple phrase or sentence). Familiarity with the correct formation of all patterns and letters is expected.

6 Pattern practice Children will need to practise the patterns at the bottom of the page. These usually reflect the pencil movement of the main activity, but always enhance fine motor control as children keep within the white lines. These patterns can be made using coloured pencils. These patterns are artwork, not letters, and should be treated as opportunities to develop movement and control.

Group work

7 Big Book page Use this with small groups to reinforce modelling the focus letters in the context of longer texts.

8 Guidance for using the Big Book page This usually includes the following sections:
- **Introduce the page** Guidance on talking about the page with children.
- **Skywriting patterns** This is based on the CD-ROM patterns.
- **Demonstrate the letter formations** This includes notes on how to involve the children interactively. Use the **Show Me** and **Get Up and Go** activities with dry-wipe boards.

Also in the Teacher's Book

9 Take away This is an additional activity which can be used for extra practice or homework. In Foundation 2 these are mostly investigative activities. In addition, each unit introducing a letter family has two Photocopy Masters (PCMs) to provide pattern practice (for children who need reinforcement at a lower level) and letter formation practice (for more confident children). The second PCM may also be used in the unit that practises the whole letter family to give extra practice of the letter formations.

10 Common errors Writing issues to look out for while children are working.

11 Out and about activity An additional activity encouraging children to look for letter patterns and shapes in the environment.

Differentiation using *Penpals* can be achieved in a number of ways:

- **Gross and fine motor skills:** younger children who are not physically ready for formal handwriting practice will benefit from the Teacher's Book suggestions for associated gross and fine motor skill activities. Some of these activities will be appropriate for the whole class while others are more suited to smaller group work with adult supervision.
- Children working individually with a teaching assistant may benefit from making patterns in trays of salt or sand in addition to working on dry-wipe boards. These children may also benefit from using the oral patter as they work.
- Take-away activities provide excellent opportunities for differentiation as detailed above. Cross-references to similar Take aways can help you to select less challenging activities for those who need extra practice at a lower level.
- Higher-achieving children can be challenged by higher expectations of control and evenness of letters.

The CD-ROM provides additional opportunities for engaging all children. The word banks offer differentiated words so that teachers may select those appropriate for individuals or groups; some words are basic CVC whilst others offer high interest.

The Practice Book page annotations in the Teacher's Book also enable you to draw the children's attention to key handwriting issues.

Assessment and record-keeping

On-going formative assessment

The most effective assessment of handwriting is on-going assessment because this gives you the chance to spot any errors or inconsistencies that are likely to impede a fast, fluent hand in the future. Be especially aware of left-handers and the difference between a pencil hold that will seriously limit their success in the future and one that has been found to work efficiently.

On the second page of every unit in the Teacher's Book, the Common errors section draws attention to the most common mistakes children make.

Record-keeping

Teacher

The best record of what children have achieved will be in the Practice Books. These provide a useful record of achievement to share with parents and colleagues.

Children

The Photocopy Master on page 9 offers a pro-forma record-keeping sheet for children. You can give them opportunities to make patterns involving straight lines, loops, circles and zig-zags, but the templates can also be adapted for other experiences, including letter formation. Photocopy a sheet, record the activity type (e.g. sand play, finger painting, construction toys) in each quadrant and date it. There is sufficient space for you to record a brief comment or for the children to make patterns, or to colour in the quadrant.

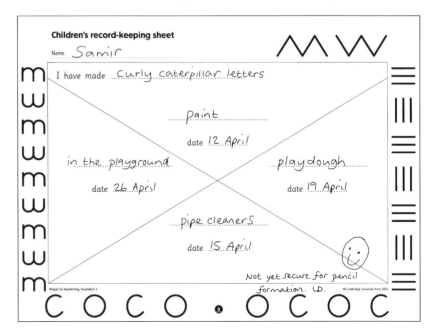

Name ....

I have made .... in

....

date ....

....

date ....

date ....

....

date ....

Glossary of key terms

Talking about handwriting

Throughout *Penpals* it has been assumed that correct terminology should be used as soon as possible. In the Foundation phase, there is an emphasis on becoming familiar with the language of the hands and the language of movement as well as talking about the letter patterns and the formation of the letters.

Terms used in *Penpals* include:

- **Gross motor skills, fine motor skills.**
- **Lower case letter.**
- **Capital letter** is used in preference to 'upper case letter'.
- **Short letter** is the term used to describe a letter with no ascender or descender.
- **Letter with an ascender.**
- **Letter with a descender.**
- **Flick** is used to describe an exit stroke (t finishes with a **curl** to the right rather than simply an exit flick).
- **Curve** is used to describe the descender on letters (y, j, g, f).
- **Cross bar** is used to describe the left-to-right line on t and f. It may also be used in relation to letters that feature a left-to-right horizontal line (e.g. e and z).
- Other important terminology used throughout *Penpals* includes: **clockwise, anticlockwise, vertical, horizontal, diagonal, parallel, joined, sloped.**

Key vocabulary

The children must be able to use and understand the following words:

- top, bottom, up, down, horizontal, vertical, diagonal, clockwise, anticlockwise.

Key CD-ROM features

- **Warm-up clips** These activities may be linked to the focus of the unit but are generally just enjoyable movement activities to warm up the muscles.
- **Sky writing** This means tracing patterns in the air, or on the carpet or table in front of you. Encourage children to use one of their fingers as a pointer for these activities.
- **Letter animation** These animations encourage the children to watch and sky write as the focus letter animates on the screen.
- **Word bank** These activities provide a useful bank of words that enable you to demonstrate the focus letter(s).
- **Show alphabet** These animations show how to form all capital and lower case letters.

In the Foundation books, certain apparatus is suggested for developing gross motor skills. Stilts, frisbees and streamers are all physical education apparatus commonly available from educational suppliers.

Letter formation

From the time children are introduced to correct letter formation during the Foundation key stage (3–5 years), there should be an expectation that they will use the correct letter formation in all the writing they do. Bad habits should not be allowed to develop. There are therefore many ideas to reinforce and practise good formation in the *Penpals* Foundation materials.

Until individual letter formation is secure, children should not be allowed to join letters.

Correct letter formation can be demonstrated using the **Show alphabet** section on the CD-ROM.

It is generally agreed that there is no right or wrong way to form capitals. However, there is a general principle of forming them from top to bottom and left to right wherever possible.

Capital Y: the use of a central stalk (as opposed to a slanting stalk) is recommended as once children have completed the 'v' form at the top of the letter, they have a clear starting point for the downwards stroke. This formation also distinguishes the capital letter from the lower case letter and retains its shape when written at speed.

Capital G: this form of G is recommended as the correct handwriting form of the letter. Variations which include a vertical line (G) are font forms.

Capital H: the formation of H using two down strokes followed by the horizontal stroke from left to right is recommended. The alternative (one down stroke followed by a horizontal and a further down stroke) can quickly resemble the letter M when written at speed.

Capital K: the formation of K with two pencil strokes rather than three is recommended as it is more fluently formed when writing at speed.

As skills and confidence develop, left-handers may well form capitals differently. This should not be an issue as capitals are never joined.

Letter patter for *Penpals*

This chart shows the oral patter for the formation of lower case and capital letters.

Long ladder family

l	Start at the top, come all the way down and flick.		L	Start at the top, come down and go across.
i	Start at the top, come down and flick. Lift and dot.		I	Start at the top, come down. Lift. Across at the top. Lift. Across at the bottom.
t	Start at the top, come all the way down and curve. Lift and cross.		T	Start at the top, come down. Lift. Across at the top.
u	Start at the top, come down and curve. Go back up, come back down and flick.		U	Start at the top, come down. Curve back up.
j	Start at the top, come all the way down and curve to the left. Lift and dot.		J	Start at the top, come down. Curve to the left. Lift. Across at the top.
y	Start at the top, come all the way down and curve. Go back up, come all the way down and curve to the left.		Y	Slope down, slope back up. Lift. Come down from the point.

One-armed robot family

r	Start at the top, come down, bounce back up and over.		R	Start at the top, come down. Lift. Back to the top. Go all the way round and slope.
b	Start at the top, come all the way down, bounce half-way back up and go all the way round.		B	Start at the top, come down. Lift. Back to the top. Go all the way round and all the way round again.
n	Start at the top, come down, bounce back up, go over, down and flick.		N	Start at the top, come down. Lift. Back to the top. Slope and straight up.
h	Start at the top, come all the way down, bounce half-way back up, go over, down and flick.		H	Start at the top, come down. Lift. Start at the top come down. Lift and across in the middle.
m	Start at the top, come down, bounce back up and over. Down, bounce back up and over. Down and flick.		M	Start at the top, come down. Lift. Back to the top. Slope down, slope up and straight down.
k or k	Start at the top, come all the way down, bounce half-way back up. Loop. Slope and flick. or Start at the top, come all the way down. Lift. Slope. Slope and flick.		K	Start at the top, come down. Lift. Slope in, slope out.
p	Start at the top, come all the way down, bounce back up and go all the way round.		P	Start at the top, come down. Lift. Back to the top. Go all the way round.

Curly caterpillar family

c	Make a curve.		C	Make a curve.
a	Make a curve, go up to the top, come back down and flick.		A	Slope to the left. Lift back to the top. Slope. Lift. Across in the middle.
d	Make a curve, go all the way up, come back down and flick.		D	Start at the top, come down. Lift. Back to the top. Go all the way round to the bottom.
o	Make a curve, go all the way round.		O	Make a curve, go all the way round.
s	Make a curve, slope, make a curve back again.		S	Make a curve, slope, make a curve back again.
g	Make a curve, go up to the top, come all the way down and curve to the left.		G	Make a curve. Lift and go across.
q	Make a curve, go up to the top, come all the way down and flick.		Q	Make a curve, go all the way round. Lift and slope across.
e	Start with a loop then make a curve.		E	Start at the top, come down. Lift. Back to the top. Across at the top. Lift. Across in the middle. Lift. Across at the bottom.
f	Make a curve, come all the way down, curve to the left. Lift and cross.		F	Start at the top, come down. Lift. Back to the top. Across at the top. Lift. Across in the middle.

Zig-zag monster family

z	Go across, slope, go back across.		Z	Go across, slope, go back across.
v	Slope down, slope back up.		V	Slope down, slope back up.
w	Slope down, slope back up. Slope down again and slope back up.		W	Slope down, slope back up. Slope down again and slope back up.
x	Slope. Lift and slope across.		X	Slope. Lift and slope across.

Pattern practice and 'play' writing are an important part of handwriting development.
Your child will be practising letter formation in a number of exciting ways: in sand,
using paint, in the air, on the interactive whiteboard as well as on paper with a pencil!
When your child is ready for letter formation, ask these questions:

- Where does the letter start?
- Is it a short letter? (a, c, e, i, m, n, o, r, s, u, v, w, x, z)
- Does it have an ascender? (b, d, f, h, k, l, t)
- Does it have a descender? (f, g, j, p, q, y)

The lower case letters are introduced in the following order in four family types:

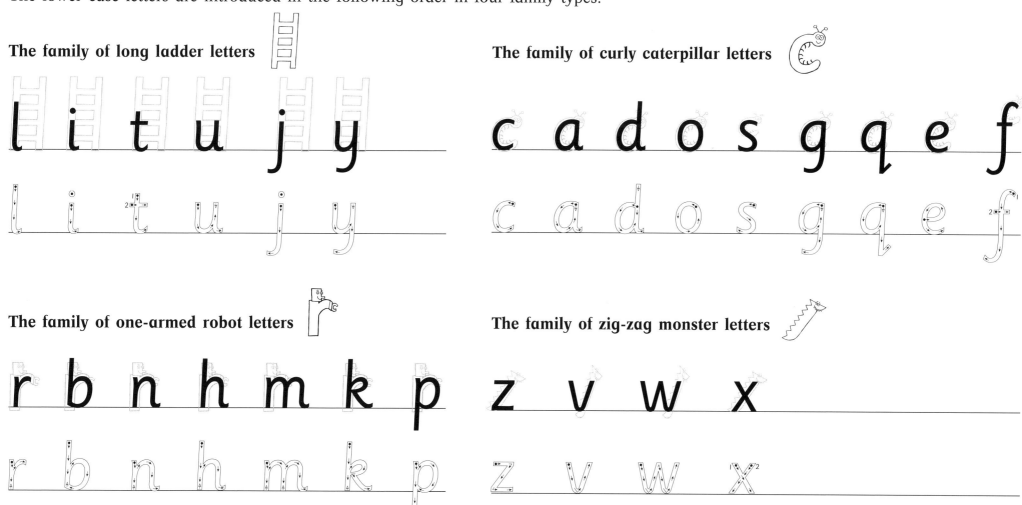

The family of long ladder letters

l i t u j y

The family of curly caterpillar letters

c a d o s g q e f

The family of one-armed robot letters

r b n h m k p

The family of zig-zag monster letters

z v w x

© Gill Budgell (Frattempo) and Kate Ruttle 2009

When you introduce *Penpals* into your school, it is important to ensure that all the staff in the school follow the scheme. To do this, it may be useful to hold an INSET staff meeting. The following pages of this book are photocopiable to make OHTs for this purpose:

- page 12 – information sheet for parents;
- inside back cover – lower case and capital letters;
- page 60 – handwriting mats.

You may also find it helpful to copy these pages from the Year 1 Teacher's Book:

- page 14 – outline of handwriting INSET session;
- page 15 – information sheet for parents;
- page 16 – font size and line width.

Suggested topics for inclusion in INSET meeting

Organisational issues

- **Rationale for introducing *Penpals*** Use the information on page 4.
- **Differentiation and record-keeping** Use the information on page 8.
- **Home–school links** Make an OHT of the information sheet on page 12.

Handwriting issues

Font Use the **Show alphabet** section on the CD-ROM or an OHT of the inside back cover of this book to demonstrate the font. Information on page 10 may be used to clarify any issues arising.

Font sizes If appropriate, photocopy Year 1 Teacher's Book page 16 to demonstrate how font size is shown throughout *Penpals*.

Writing on lined paper Children should be encouraged to write on lined paper from the time they begin to focus on correct letter formation and orientation. As the children's handwriting becomes more controlled, the depth between the lines should decrease. It may well be that at any given time different children in your class will benefit from writing on paper with different line depths. The size of the font in the Practice Books is intended to reflect a development in handwriting. However, you should still tailor the handwriting materials to meet the needs of individual children in your class.

Some children may prefer to write on lined paper which also includes guidelines for the height of ascenders and descenders.

Pencil hold Use the photos and video clips on the CD-ROM to discuss the importance of pencil hold and posture with parents. However, there are many alternative pencil holds (particularly for left-handers) and the most important thing is comfort and a hold that will be efficient under speed. Some children may benefit from triangular pencils or ordinary pencils with plastic pencil grips.

Posture A good posture and pencil hold are vital for good handwriting. Although many young children enjoy sitting on one foot, kneeling or wrapping their feet around the legs of the chair, they will find it easier to sustain good handwriting comfortably if they adopt a good posture.

Left-handed children Left-handed children should not sit to the right of right-handed children as their papers will meet in the middle! Left-handed children should be taught to position their paper to the left of centre and then angle the paper for comfort as suggested below. There is no reason why left-handed children's handwriting should be any worse than that of right-handed children.

Sloped surfaces Children who experience some motor control difficulties often benefit from writing on a slight slope. The easiest and cheapest way to provide this in the classroom is to use substantial A4 or foolscap ring-binders of which there are usually plenty in school. Commercial wooden or plastic writing slopes are also widely available.

Angle of paper: using the writing mats Make an OHT of the writing mat for right- and left-handed children as provided on page 60. You can photocopy these onto A3 paper, mount them on card and laminate them to make table-top mats for the children. Use the spaces provided to allow children to find the optimum position.

Show the children how to line up the corners of their books to create a comfortable angle for writing, or how to use Blu-tack to secure lined paper to the mats. Encourage the children to explore personal variation of the angles.

Remind the children that they need to move their paper as they change from left- to right-hand pages!

Unit focus: introducing the long ladder letter family.
Phonic links: hearing initial phoneme l; alliteration in *long ladder*.

Letter animation
Talk about the long ladder family mnemonic. Play the letter animation and say the patter. Children make the letter shape and say the patter.

Sky writing
Children copy the three patterns which emphasise movements in the long ladder family. Say "Start at the top, come down." as children begin each movement.

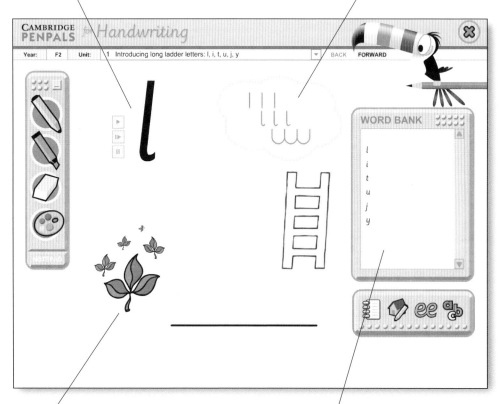

Challenge artwork
The picture illustrates a word beginning with the target letter. Children identify the picture word (leaf). Write the word and establish the target letter.

Word bank
Choose a letter to discuss. Click on the letter to make it grey. Model and discuss the movements needed to form the letter.

Gross motor skills
- Children walk tall.
- Children stretch out on the floor.
- Children stretch up, then slowly fold down (link to music and movement).

Fine motor skills
- Children make play dough long ladder shapes. Then they trace them with a finger.
- Children weave with paper strips.
- Children thread strings of beads.
- Children arrange strips of paper to make long ladders.

Play and practise

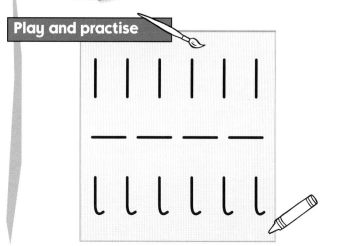

14

✋ Children practise sky writing long ladder patterns.

Independent work

1 Identify the unit title.

2 Children finger trace these letters saying the sound.

3 Remind the children to use the oral patter.

6 Can the children identify the pictures and the initial phoneme? Can they spot the double l in the middle of *lollipop*? Children read the words and then trace the ls.

7 Children write the missing ls in the spaces. Can they think of another word beginning with l?

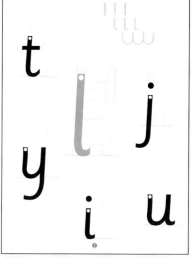

Big Book page 2

Practice Book 1 pages 2–3

4 Check pencil holds while children pencil trace over the letters.

5 Check correct letter formation as children write the letter independently.

8 Children write a line of ls. Check for pencil hold and correct letter formation.

9 Children trace over the patterns.

Common errors

- not starting at the top
- omitting the flick
- reversing the flick
- letters not sitting on the line

Out and about activity

Go for a walk to look for long ladder shapes (e.g. drainpipes, climbing frames, corners of buildings, gate posts). Ask the children to stretch up and trace the shape down to the ground.

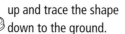

Take away

Children use **PCM 1 or 2** as long ladder family pattern or letter practice.

Introduce the page
- Encourage the children to talk about the page before you begin.
- Point out the long ladder artwork.

Skywriting patterns
- Emphasise always starting at the top, coming down. Exaggerate no flick/flick.

Demonstrate the letter formations
- Demonstrate the long ladder pattern using the ladder picture and the oral letter family patter (see page 11).
- Emphasise the starting point and exit flick, and use the patter.
- Demonstrate the rest of the letters.
  Get Up and Go Ask the children to point to the starting point of each letter in the family.
  Show Me Children practise the letter l.
- Ask children to put the letters into sets. (t and l have ascenders, j and y have descenders, i and u are short.)
- Note that the descenders curve to the left on j and y.
- Look at the two short letters in this family, u and i.

15

CD-ROM

Unit focus: introducing i as a short letter in relation to l as a letter with an ascender.
Phonic link: hearing initial phoneme l.

Letter animations
Choose a letter. Play the letter animation and say the patter. Children make the letter shape and say the patter.

Sky writing
Children copy the three patterns which emphasise movements in the long ladder family. Say "Start at the top, come down." as children begin each movement.

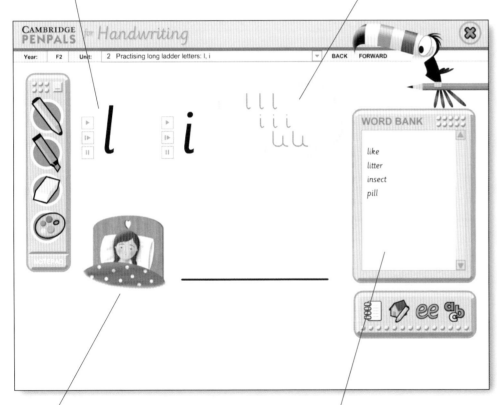

Challenge artwork
The picture illustrates a word that features both target letters. Children identify the picture word (ill). Write the word and establish the target letters.

Word bank
Choose a word to discuss. Click on the word to make the target graphemes grey. Model and discuss the letter formation and phonemes.

Gross motor skills
- Children walk tall.
- Children bend knees and walk at half height.
- Children curl into a ball, then jump up high and punch the air.
- Children practise walking tall on stilts.

Fine motor skills
- Children draw long and short lines in sand or chalk in the playground.
- Children make tall and short towers with building blocks.
- Children cut along tall and short straight lines from the base of a piece of paper.

Play and practise

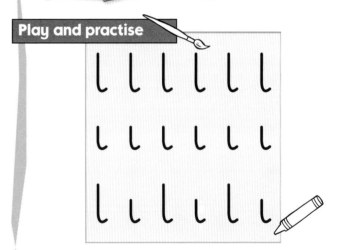

Practice Book warm up

✋ Children practise the long and short ladder patterns.

Independent work

Identify the unit title.
❶

Children finger trace these letters saying the sounds.
❷

Remind the children about the tall l and the short i.
❸

Can the children identify the pictures and the initial phonemes? Can they finish off the lollipop sticks, starting at the top? They read the word and then trace the ls.
❻

Children write the missing ls and i in the spaces.
❼

Big Book page 3

Practice Book 1 pages 4–5

❹ Check pencil holds while children pencil trace over the letters.

❺ Check correct letter formation as children write the letters independently.

❽ Children write a line of lis. Check for pencil hold and correct letter formation.

❾ Children trace over the patterns, talking about the difference in height.

Introduce the page

- Encourage the children to talk about the page before you begin.
- Talk about the pictures and talk about the initial phoneme l.

Skywriting patterns

- Emphasise tall and short ladders. Have fun with the dots!

Demonstrate the letter formations

- Talk about the height of the letters – tall and short.
- Point out that both letters are sitting on the line.
- Trace over l and i, emphasising the letter formation.
- Talk about the dot on the i.
  Show Me Children practise each letter in turn.
  Get Up and Go Ask the children to point to the is and ls in all the words as you trace over them.

Common errors

- not starting at the top
- omitting the flick
- letters not sitting on the line
- not differentiating the height

Out and about activity

Chalk one of the skywriting patterns onto the playground. Ask children to run up and down the tall and short lines.

Take away

Children find long and short pairs of objects (e.g. cutlery, sticks, flower stems, pencils), talk about them at home and bring them into school for sharing.

CD-ROM

Unit focus: introducing u as a short letter in relation to t as a letter with an ascender. Note also that t has a curl rather than an exit flick.
Phonic links: hearing initial phoneme **t**; reading CVC words.

Letter animations
Choose a letter. Play the letter animation and say the patter. Children make the letter shape and say the patter.

Sky writing
Children copy the three patterns which emphasise movements in the long ladder family. Identify vertical and horizontal lines in the patterns.

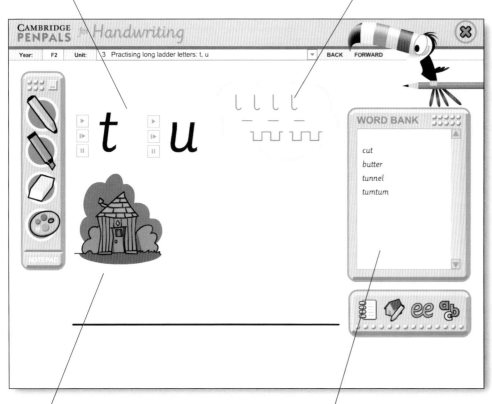

Challenge artwork
The picture illustrates a word that features both target letters. Children identify the picture word (hut). Write the word and establish the target letters.

Word bank
Choose a word to discuss. Click on the word to make the target graphemes grey. Model and discuss the letter formation and phonemes.

Gross motor skills
- Children practise the flick wrist action using frisbees (or paper plates) or streamers.
- Children make their bodies into a t. They will need to work with a partner to make the curl at the bottom.

Fine motor skills
- Children decorate outlines of t and u with vertical and horizontal lines.

- Children make criss-cross patterns with thin strips of paper. Emphasise the vertical and horizontal.
- Children make a long line using bricks.

Play and practise

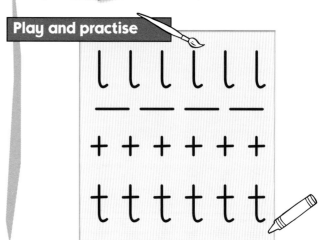

Big Book page 4

Practice Book warm up

- Children remember the long ladder pattern and sky write it.
- Children move their fingers as if they were hunting for nuts.

Independent work

1 Identify the unit title and objective.

2 Children finger trace these letters, saying the sounds.

3 Remind the children about the short u and tall t.

6 Can the children identify the pictures?

7 Read the sentence together. Children find the letters u and t and trace over them. How many nuts can they find on the page? (5)

Practicing long ladder letters: t, u

Finger trace. Say the sounds.

u t ut ut

Pencil trace.

Write.

Read and write.

H nt he n ts.

Trace the patterns.

9 Children trace over the patterns. Make further patterns inside the squirrel.

Practice Book 1 pages 6–7

4 Check pencil holds while children pencil trace over the letters.

5 Check correct letter formation as children write the letters independently.

8 Children write a line of uts. Check for pencil hold and correct letter formation. Talk about the difference in height between these letters.

Common errors

- not starting at the top
- omitting the flick or curl

u t

- incorrect formation of the t (e.g. adding the curl at the end, after the pencil lift)
- not retracing the line on the way down the u

U

Out and about activity

Go for a walk and ask children to look out for examples of horizontal and vertical lines crossing (e.g. fences, window frames, railway tracks).

Take away

Children find ts and us in magazines and newspapers. Children could bring them into school and stick them onto giant t and u outlines.

Introduce the page

- Encourage the children to talk about the page. Talk about the pictures. Establish that they all show people doing naughty things, so we say "Tut tut".
- Talk about the exclamation mark and the capital T.
- Identify the initial phoneme **t**.
- NB: there is potential for pattern practice in the artwork.

Skywriting patterns

- Emphasise the horizontal and then the vertical lines.

Demonstrate the letter formations

- Trace over u and t, emphasising letter formation.
- Talk about the height of the letters – tall and short.
- Both letters are sitting on the line but u has a flick and t has a curl.
- Talk about the horizontal cross bar on the t and its left-to-right formation. Demonstrate that the cross bar goes on last, after a pencil lift.
  Show Me Children practise each letter in turn.
- Trace over the words *Tut tut*.

CD-ROM

Unit focus: introducing j and y as letters with descenders.
Phonic link: hearing initial phonemes **j** and **y**.

Letter animations
Choose a letter. Play the letter animation and say the patter. Children make the letter shape and say the patter.

Sky writing
Children copy the three patterns which emphasise movements in the long ladder family. For the first two patterns say "Start at the top, come down." as children begin each movement.

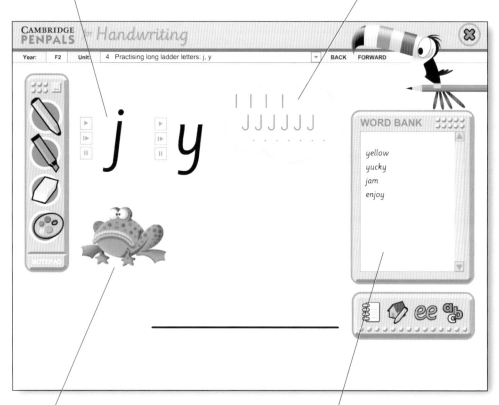

Challenge artwork
The picture illustrates a word that features both target letters. Children identify the picture word (jumpy). Write the word and establish the target letters.

Word bank
Choose a word to discuss. Click on the word to make the target graphemes grey. Model and discuss the letter formation and phonemes.

Gross motor skills
- Children mime using a yoyo. This is excellent for reinforcing up and down arm movements.
- Children make skipping ropes into ys and js. Coil a rope to represent the dot over the j.

Fine motor skills
- Children fill in outlines of a j and a y by painting dots using cotton buds or their fingertips.

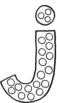

- Children try lacing cards to reinforce the idea of going down and back up again.

Play and practise

Practice Book warm up

- Children practise the long ladder pattern.
- Children practise the long ladder pattern with a curve to the left at the bottom.

Independent work

1 Identify the unit title. You can choose to work across the page dealing with j and y together or you can work through j first and then y.

2 Children finger trace these letters, saying the sounds.

3 Check pencil holds while children pencil trace over the letters. Remind the children about the long descender.

6 Read the phrase together. Children find the letters j and y and trace over them.

7 Children write the missing js and ys in the spaces.

9 Children trace over the patterns.

Practice Book 1 pages 8–9

4 Check correct letter formation as children write the letters independently.

5 Can the children identify the picture?

8 Children write a line of js and then ys. Check for pencil hold and correct letter formation. Talk about these letters both having a long descender and the j having a dot.

Common errors

- not starting at the top
- not positioning the descender under the line
- curving the descender the wrong way

Take away

Children practise left and right.

Your left hand makes an **L** shape, so it's your **Left**.

Your right hand **doesn't** make an **L** shape, so it's your right.

Out and about activity

Ask children to search for dot patterns in the environment (e.g. fabric patterns, wallpaper, plasterwork). They can try dot rubbings from manhole covers or textured flooring, for example.

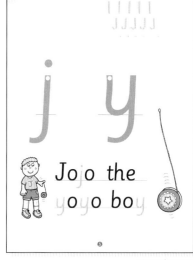

Big Book page 5

Introduce the page

- Encourage the children to talk about the page.
- Talk about the picture and the patterns on the yoyo.
- Mention the capital J and remind children that we use a capital letter for names. Use the inside back cover of the Big Book to show all the capitals if appropriate.
- Identify the initial phonemes **j** and **y**.

Skywriting patterns

- Emphasise the curve to the left (the direction of the j and y descender).

Demonstrate the letter formations

- Trace over the j and the y, emphasising the letter formation.
- Both letters have descenders and they both curve to the left.
- Point out that j has a dot over it. Ask the children: can you think of another letter that has a dot over it? (i)
- Talk about the position of the letters on the line. **Show Me** Children practise each letter in turn.
- Trace over the letters in the phrase.

CD-ROM

Unit focus: revisiting all the long ladder letters in context.
Phonic links: recognising all the letters in the long ladder family as letters and phonemes.

Letter animations
Choose a letter. Play the letter animation and say the patter. Children make the letter shape and say the patter.

Words
Click on a word to make the target graphemes grey. Model and discuss the letter formation and phonemes.

Challenge artwork
The picture illustrates a word that features some of the target letters. Children identify the picture word (juggling). Write the word and establish the target letters.

Gross motor skills
- Children roll hoops to practise a forward propelling action.
- Children use stilts – the type that look like upside-down flowerpots. This develops strength and tone in lower arm muscles as children pull the ropes upwards to hold them taut.

Fine motor skills
- Children cut straight lines.
- Children cut out an umbrella shape.

Play and practise

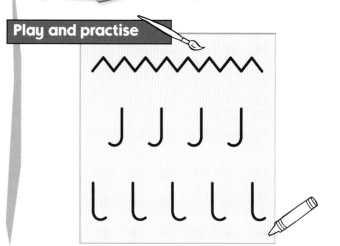

Big Book page 6

Practice Book warm up

- Practise the long ladder pattern.
- Practise straight lines curving to the left and then to the right.

Independent work

Identify the unit title.
1

Children pencil trace the first letter of each line and then complete the line independently. Revise the oral patter if necessary.
2

Remind the children about short and tall letters and letters with descenders. Remind them about the position and left-to-right direction of the cross bar on the t.
3

Check correct letter formation and pencil hold as children write the letters independently.
4

Children trace over the handles of the umbrellas. Note which ones curve to the left (like a y or a j) and which ones curl to the right (like a t).
5

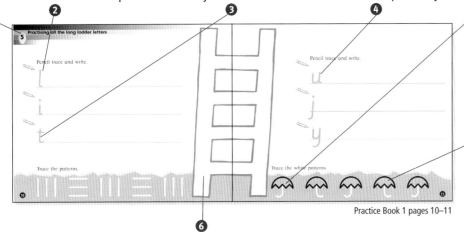

Children trace over the patterns at the bottom of both pages.
7

Practice Book 1 pages 10–11

Children decorate the ladder with patterns of letters from the long ladder family. Encourage pattern-making rather than simple colouring.
6

Common errors

- flicks too large
- descenders too long or above the line
- curving the descender the wrong way

- incorrect relative heights of short and tall letters
- using a flick for the curl of t

Take away

Children can use (or re-use) **PCM 2** according to their individual practice needs.

Out and about activity

Encourage children to look at print in the environment. They can make a simple chart, search for long ladder letters and tick the chart each time they see one.

23

Introduce the page

- Begin by recapping the letters in the long ladder family (l, i, t, u, j, y).
- Encourage the children to talk about the page and the patterns in the pictures.
- Talk about the picture and read the words. Identify the initial phonemes. Ask the children: how do you think the party entertainer makes the yellow bugs appear from under the jug? Brief discussion may follow!

  Get Up and Go Invite the children to find the examples of each letter in the long ladder family.
- Remind the children of the correct formation as you trace over the letters in the phrases.

  Show Me Children practise each letter in turn.

CD-ROM

Unit focus: introducing the one-armed robot letter family.
Phonic link: hearing initial phoneme **r**.

Letter animation
Talk about the one-armed robot family mnemonic. Play the letter animation and say the patter. Children make the letter shape and say the patter.

Sky writing
Children copy the three patterns which emphasise movements in the one-armed robot family. Say "Start at the top, come down, bounce back up and over." as children begin each movement.

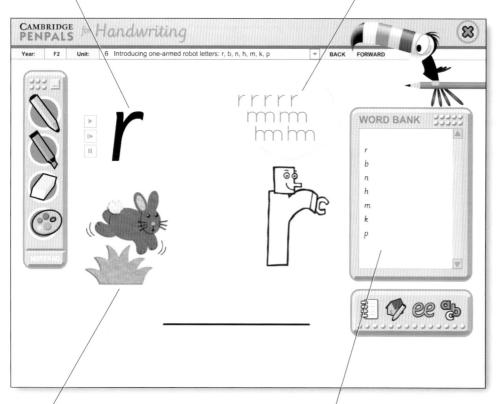

Challenge artwork
The picture illustrates a word beginning with the target letter. Children identify the picture word (rabbit). Write the word and establish the target letter.

Word bank
Choose a letter to discuss. Click on the letter to make it grey. Model and discuss the movements needed to form the letter.

Gross motor skills
- Children practise jumping up and down.
- Children practise bouncing balls with a flat palm.
- If space and equipment are available, children practise bouncing while sitting on large balls or space hoppers.
- Children bunny hop across the floor to encourage awareness of the 'bouncing back up' pattern.

Fine motor skills
- Children make long Plasticine sausages and then shape them into one-armed robot patterns. It may be easier to draw the pattern on a laminated card and encourage children to lay the Plasticine on top.
- Develop the pincer movement. Put out a selection of clothes pegs and encourage the children to make patterns with them by clipping them onto strips of card or lollipop sticks.

Play and practise

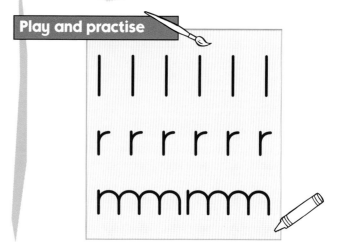

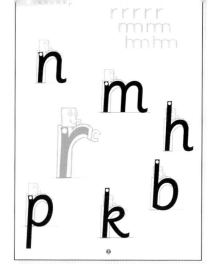

Big Book page 7

Practice Book warm up

Children practise sky writing one-armed robot patterns.

Independent work

1 Identify the unit title.

2 Children finger trace these letters, saying the sound.

3 Remind the children to use the oral patter.

6 Can the children identify the pictures and the **r** phonemes (in *roar* and *robot*)? They read the words and then trace the *r*s.

7 Children write the missing *r*s in the spaces.

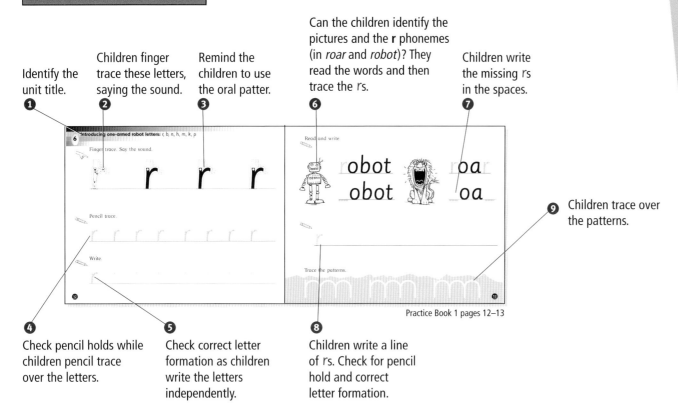

9 Children trace over the patterns.

Practice Book 1 pages 12–13

4 Check pencil holds while children pencil trace over the letters.

5 Check correct letter formation as children write the letters independently.

8 Children write a line of *r*s. Check for pencil hold and correct letter formation.

Common errors

- not starting at the top
- not retracing the downward stroke
- exaggerating the arch

Out and about activity

Ask children to look for arch shapes (e.g. over doors, in trees, windows, bridges).

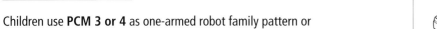

Take away

Children use **PCM 3 or 4** as one-armed robot family pattern or letter practice.

Introduce the page

- Encourage the children to talk about the page before you begin.
- Point out the one-armed robot artwork.

Skywriting patterns

- Emphasise bouncing back up as you retrace the line each time.

Demonstrate the letter formations

- Demonstrate the one-armed robot pattern using the robot picture and the oral letter family patter (see page 11).
- Emphasise the starting point.
- Ask the children to make sets with the letters. Some letters are short (r, n, m), some have ascenders (k, b, h) and one has a descender (p).
- Note which letters have an exit flick (n, m, h and k).
- Demonstrate forming the rest of the letters.
  Get Up and Go Ask the children to point to the starting point of each letter in the family.
  Show Me Children practise the letter r.

CD-ROM

Unit focus: introducing b as a letter with an ascender and n as a short letter.
Phonic link: hearing initial phonemes **b** and **n**.

Letter animations
Choose a letter. Play the letter animation and say the patter. Children make the letter shape and say the patter.

Sky writing
Children copy the three patterns which emphasise movements in the one-armed robot family. Where appropriate, say "Start at the top, come down, bounce back up and over." as children begin each movement.

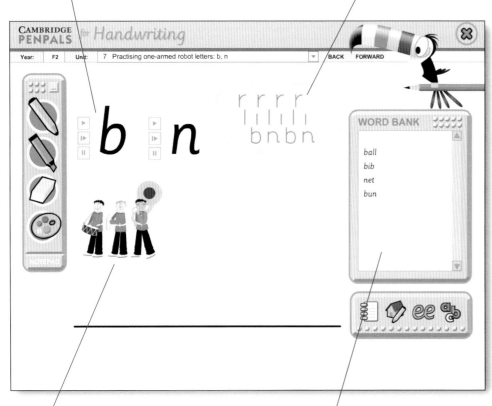

Challenge artwork
The picture illustrates a word that features both target letters. Children identify the picture word (band). Write the word and establish the target letters.

Word bank
Choose a word to discuss. Click on the word to make the target graphemes grey. Model and discuss the letter formation and phonemes.

Gross motor skills
- Children use frisbees (or paper plates) to practise a sweeping arm movement.
- Children climb high and low.

Fine motor skills
- Children cut along short and long lines.

- Children make buns out of play dough, kneading, prodding, rolling and bashing the dough.
- Children stick buttons on to a b shape. Talk about colour, texture and pattern.

Play and practise

Practice Book warm up

✋ Children practise long and short one-armed robot patterns.

Independent work

1 Identify the unit title. You can choose to work across the page dealing with b and n together or you can work through b and then n.

2 Children finger trace these letters, saying the sounds.

5 Can the children identify the pictures?

6 Read the phrase together. Children find the letters b and n and trace over them.

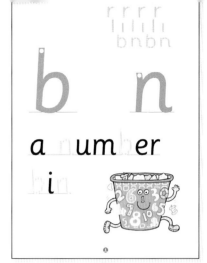

Big Book page 8

8 Children trace over the patterns and trace the rabbit's route across the top of the letters. (Children who finish early can fill in the rabbits with blue patterns.)

Practice Book 1 pages 14–15

3 Check pencil holds while children pencil trace over the letters. Remind the children about the ascender on the b and that n is a short letter.

4 Check correct letter formation as children write the letters independently.

7 Children write a line of bs and then ns. Check for pencil hold and correct letter formation. Talk about the difference in height between these letters.

Common errors

- not starting at the top
- confusing n and h
- not bouncing back so b looks like a number 6
- incorrect relative heights (the bulge on the b should be the same height as the n)

bn

Take away

At home, children make a collection of things that begin with b.

bag

Out and about activity

Children write *bin* labels for the classroom or school bins and stick them on. Are there numbers around the school? Which ones can the children find?

Introduce the page

- Encourage the children to talk about the page before you begin.
- Talk about the picture and the numbers. Then talk about the initial phonemes **n** and **b** in the phrase.

Skywriting patterns

- Emphasise the difference between tall and short patterns. Have fun with the bouncing back up!

Demonstrate the letter formations

- Trace over the b and the n, emphasising the letter formation.
- Talk about the height of the letters – tall and short.
- Both letters are sitting on the line.
- Note that n has an exit flick but b does not.
  Show Me Children practise each letter in turn.
  Get Up and Go Ask the children to point to the bs and ns in the phrase *a number bin*.
- Trace over the ns and bs in each word.
- Note that there is an incidental opportunity here to teach the formation of numerals 1–10 if this is appropriate.

CD-ROM

Unit focus: introducing h as a letter with an ascender and m as a short letter.
Phonic link: hearing initial phonemes **h** and **m**.

Letter animations
Choose a letter. Play the letter animation and say the patter. Children make the letter shape and say the patter.

Sky writing
Children copy the three patterns which emphasise movements in the one-armed robot family. Where appropriate, say "Start at the top, come down, bounce back up and over." as children begin each movement.

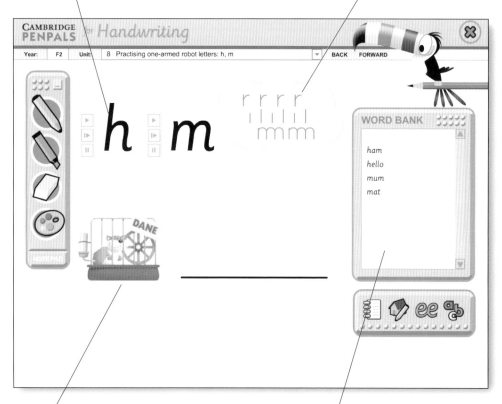

Challenge artwork
The picture illustrates a word that features both target letters. Children identify the picture word (hamster). Write the word and establish the target letters.

Word bank
Choose a word to discuss. Click on the word to make the target graphemes grey. Model and discuss the letter formation and phonemes.

Gross motor skills
● Spread some large sheets of paper on the floor. Encourage children to make large 'bouncing back up' patterns using paint or felt tips.
● Children use ribbons or streamers to make high waves by standing up tall, and low waves by crouching down.

Fine motor skills
● Children thread pasta tubes on to short and long pieces of string to make necklaces.
● Children model letter shapes with pipe cleaners. (If necessary make shapes on paper or laminated card for children to overlay.)
● Make Plasticine one-armed robot shapes.

Play and practise

Children practise one-armed robot patterns.

Independent work

① Identify the unit title. You can choose to work across the page dealing with h and m together or you can work through h and then m.

② Children finger trace these letters, saying the sounds.

⑤ Can the children identify the picture?

⑥ Read the phrase together. Children find the letters h and m and trace over them.

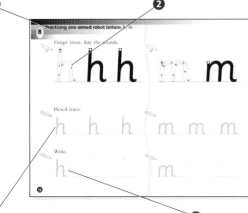

Practice Book 1 pages 16–17

⑧ Children trace over the patterns running across the top of the pictures.

③ Check pencil holds while children pencil trace over the letters. Remind the children about the ascender on the h and that m is a short letter.

④ Check correct letter formation as children write the letters independently.

⑦ Children write a line of ms and then hs. Check for pencil hold and correct letter formation. Talk about the difference in height between these letters.

Common errors

- not starting at the top
- not making the arches of the m regular

- incorrect relative heights (the hump of the h should be the same height as the m)

Take away

Children practise writing *mum* and *mummy*.

Out and about activity

Take some chalk outside and make huge hs and mega ms for the children to run around. Make sure they start at the correct place and retrace their steps as necessary.

29

Big Book page 9

Introduce the page

- Encourage the children to talk about the page before you begin.
- Identify the diagram and the labels and talk about the initial phonemes **h** and **m**. Can the children find the m at the end of *arm*?

Skywriting patterns

- Emphasise the tall and short shapes and the up and down patterns.

Demonstrate the letter formations

- Trace over the h and the m, emphasising the letter formation.
- Talk about the relative height of the letters – h has an ascender and m is a short letter.
- Both letters are sitting on the line.
- Both letters have an exit flick.
  Show Me Children practise each letter in turn.
  Get Up and Go Ask the children to point to the hs and ms in the labels.
- Trace over the ms and hs in each word.

CD-ROM

Unit focus: introducing k as a letter with an ascender and p as a letter with a straight descender.

Phonic link: hearing initial phonemes **k** and **p**.

Letter animations
Choose a letter. Play the letter animation and say the patter. Children make the letter shape and say the patter.

Sky writing
Children copy the three patterns which emphasise movements in the one-armed robot family. For the first pattern say "Start at the top, come down, bounce back up and over." as children begin each movement.

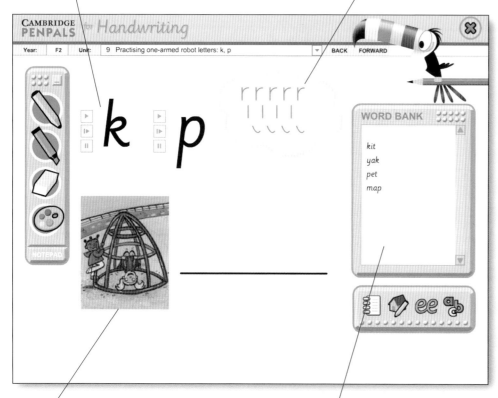

Challenge artwork
The picture illustrates a word that features both target letters. Children identify the picture word (park). Write the word and establish the target letters.

Word bank
Choose a word to discuss. Click on the word to make the target graphemes grey. Model and discuss the letter formation and phonemes.

Gross motor skills
- Children run in circles in the playground, first clockwise and then anticlockwise.
- Children propel hoops across the hall to encourage a pushing-off arm movement.
- Children practise bunny hopping.

Fine motor skills
- Children fill in outlines of a p with spirals and circles drawn clockwise from the centre.

- Children work on the pincer movement, picking up ks and ps from a selection of sequinned letters. (These letters are available from greetings card shops for celebrating birthdays.)

Play and practise

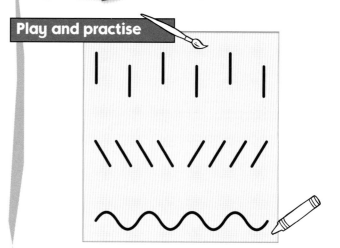

Practice Book warm up

✋ Children practise down, up and over movements with their hands.

✋ Children stretch up tall and bend down low.

Independent work

1 Identify the unit title. You can choose to work across the page dealing with k and p together or you can work through k and then p.

2 Children finger trace these letters, saying the sounds.

5 Can the children identify the picture?

6 Read the instruction together. Children find the letters k and p and trace over them. At this point or later, children can fill in the king with pink patterns!

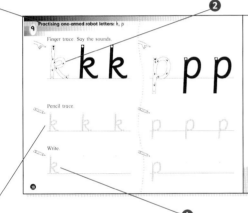

Practice Book 1 pages 18–19

8 Children trace over the pattern that weaves between the pictures.

3 Check pencil holds while children pencil trace over the letters. Remind the children about the descender of the p and about the ascender on the k and the height of its loop.

4 Check correct letter formation as children write the letters independently.

7 Children write a line of ks and then ps. Check for pencil hold and correct letter formation. Talk about the difference between these letters (one has an ascender and one has a descender).

Common errors

- making the loop of the k too large, so that it looks like a capital R

- not sitting the p on the line with the descender below the line

Out and about activity

Ask children to look out for examples of ks and ps on signs around the school and in the street.

Take away

Children make a collection of pink things and label them *pink*.

Introduce the page

- Encourage the children to talk about the page before you begin.
- Talk about the picture and the initial phonemes **k** and **p**. Discuss the patterns in the picture.
- Invite the children to think of another animal beginning with p (e.g. panther, parrot) and with k (e.g. koala, kitten).

Skywriting patterns

- Emphasise the bouncing back up and over, and the flick on the diagonal stroke (like the flick on the k).

Demonstrate the letter formations

- Trace over the k and the p, emphasising the letter formation.
- Talk about the height of the ascender on the letter k. The k sits on the line and it has an exit flick.
- Talk about the fact that the loop of the k is the same height as the top of the p.
- Talk about the descender of the p.
  Show Me Children practise each letter in turn.
  Get Up and Go Ask the children to point to the k and p in the phrase *king penguin*.
- Trace over the k and p in the phrase.

CD-ROM

Unit focus: revisiting all the one-armed robot letters in context.
Phonic link: recognising all the letters in the one-armed robot family as letters and phonemes.

Letter animations
Choose a letter. Play the letter animation and say the patter. Children make the letter shape and say the patter.

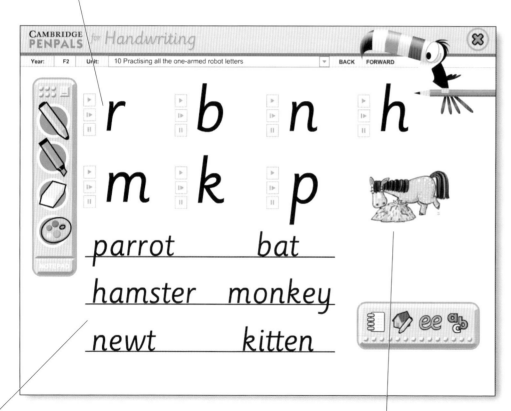

CAMBRIDGE PENPALS *for Handwriting*

Year: F2   Unit: 10 Practising all the one-armed robot letters   BACK   FORWARD

r   b   n   h
m   k   p

parrot   bat

hamster   monkey

newt   kitten

Words
Click on a word to make the target graphemes grey. Model and discuss the letter formation and phonemes.

Challenge artwork
The picture illustrates a word that features some of the target letters. Children identify the picture word (horse). Write the word and establish the target letters.

Gross motor skills
- Children use ribbons or streamers to practise all the one-armed robot letter patterns.
- Children walk like robots with stiff limbs. They then pretend to float like feathers as a contrast.
- Children make a large circle, all holding hands. They move in a clockwise and then anticlockwise direction.

Fine motor skills
- Using a different colour or writing implement, children fill in an outline of a rabbit, completing each section with a different letter.

- Children trace each one-armed robot letter in sand or paint.

Play and practise

👆 Children sing *Here Is The Church* and do the actions to stretch their fingers (see **Foundation 1 CD, track 17; Teacher's Book, page 46**).

Independent work

① Identify the unit title.

② Children pencil trace the first letter of each line and then complete the line independently. Revise the oral patter if necessary.

④ Check correct letter formation and pencil hold as children write the letters independently.

⑤ Children trace over the patterns at the bottom of both pages and, if time, make a pattern in the bottom layer of the wall.

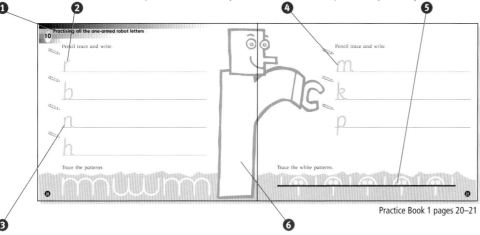

Practice Book 1 pages 20–21

③ Remind the children about short letters, letters with ascenders and letters with descenders.

⑥ If time, children may like to decorate the robot with patterns of letters from this family. Encourage pattern-making rather than simple colouring.

Common errors

- not starting at the top
- too large an exit flick
- too high or low an ascender on the b, h and k
- too long or short a descender on the p
- incorrect relative heights
- not bouncing back up

h k m

b h k

p p

h r n

Out and about activity

Ask children to look at environmental print. They can search for one-armed robot letters and make a simple chart to tick each time they see one.

Take away

Children can use (or re-use) **PCM 4** according to their individual practice needs.

Big Book page 11

Introduce the page

- Begin by recapping the letters in the one-armed robot family (r, b, n, h, m, k, p).
- Encourage the children to talk about the page.
- Identify what is happening in the picture and read the words. Ask the children: why do you think the rabbits are running home so quickly?
  Get Up and Go Invite the children to find the examples of each letter in the sentence following the sequence shown in the box at the top of the page.
- Remind the children of the correct formation as you trace over the letters.
  Show Me Children practise each letter in turn.

CD-ROM

Unit focus: introducing capital letters for letters in the one-armed robot family.

Phonic links: reinforcing initial phonemes associated with capitals and lower case letters r, b, n, h, m, k and p; ensuring that children understand that capital and lower case letters represent the same phonemes.

Letter animations

Choose a letter. Play the letter animation and say the patter.
Children make the letter shape and say the patter. Ask children to show the lower case equivalent of the letter.

Challenge artwork

The picture features a group of children with names beginning with the target letter. Children guess the names. Write the names and establish the target letter.

Word bank

Choose a name to discuss. Click on the name to make the capital letter grey. Model and discuss the movements needed to form the letter.

Gross motor skills

- Children roll hoops to encourage a forward propelling action.
- Children sing *In And Out The Dusty Bluebells* (see **Foundation 1 CD, track 21; Teacher's Book, page 46**) and make arches with their arms for others to skip through.
- Children use ribbons or streamers to make clockwise circles in the air.

Fine motor skills

- Prepare a laminated A4 card with capital letters drawn on it in marker pen. Children roll out Plasticine and model the shapes by placing the Plasticine on top.

Play and practise

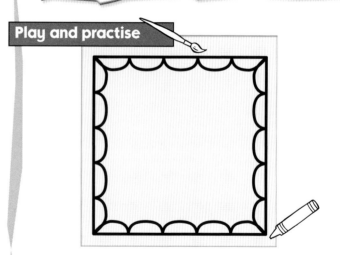

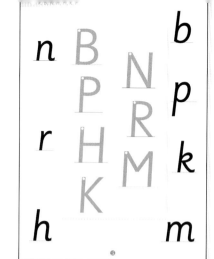

Big Book page 12

Practice Book warm up

👐 Children contrast clockwise and anticlockwise finger patterns using each finger and each hand in turn.
👐 Children circle their shoulders clockwise and then anticlockwise.

Independent work

Identify the unit title. We suggest that each letter is finger traced and then practised in turn.

Children finger trace each capital, saying the sounds.

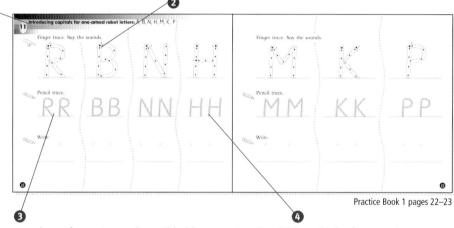

Practice Book 1 pages 22–23

1 Check correct letter formation and pencil hold as children first trace and then write the letters independently. Encourage them to finger trace and pencil trace each letter several times.

4 Can the children think of names that begin with these letters? (e.g. Bella, Puja, Rajiv, Nick, Helen, Maria, Karl)

Common errors

- letters too big
- not meeting initial vertical
- not starting at the top
- bouncing back up the main line
- K – not connecting the < to the |

 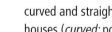

Take away

Children write the name of their street in capitals (copying from the street sign).

Out and about activity

Ask the children to look for curved and straight shapes in houses (*curved:* pots, ironwork, curtains, hanging baskets; *straight:* doors, window frames, tiles, roofs).

Introduce the page

- Encourage the children to talk about the page before you begin.
- Identify the fact that it is a matching game. Talk about the letter shapes and phonemes.
- Talk about when you would use capitals (beginnings of sentences, names).

Demonstrate the letter formations

- Talk about the fact that all these letters are different in their lower case and capital forms (p's difference lies in its position relative to the baseline).
- Talk about how many pencil strokes it takes to make each letter. (All of them are written with two strokes except H, which is written with three.)
  Show Me Children practise each capital letter in turn.
  Get Up and Go Ask the children to match the capitals to the lower case letters by drawing a line between the two.

CD-ROM

Unit focus: introducing capital letters for letters in the long ladder family.

Phonic links: recognising phonemes associated with capitals and lower case letters l, i, t, u, j, y; ensuring that children understand that capital and lower case letters represent the same phonemes.

Letter animations

Choose a letter. Play the letter animation and say the patter. Children make the letter shape and say the patter. Ask children to show the lower case equivalent of the letter.

Challenge artwork

The picture features a group of children with names beginning with the target letter. Children guess the names. Write the names and establish the target letter.

Word bank

Choose a name to discuss. Click on the name to make the capital letter grey. Model and discuss the movements needed to form the letter.

Gross motor skills

- Children walk tall.
- Children stretch out on the floor.
- Children stretch up and then slowly fold down.

Fine motor skills

- Children make play dough capital letter shapes.
- Children make these capital letter shapes using bricks (only U and J need curves).
- Children weave with paper strips.
- Children thread strings of beads.

Play and practise

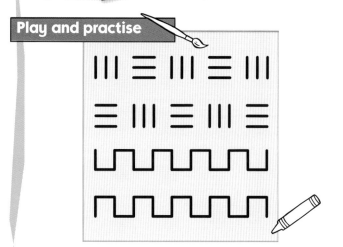

☝ Children sing *Firework* (see **Foundation 1 CD, track 20; Teacher's Book, page 46**) and make their fingers move like the sparks and the flames.

☝ Children move their shoulders up towards their ears, first on one side, then the other.

Independent work

Children finger trace each capital, saying the sounds.
2

❸ Check correct letter formation and pencil hold as children first trace and then write the letters independently. Encourage them to finger trace and pencil trace each letter several times.

❶ Identify the unit title. We suggest that each letter is finger traced and then practised in turn.

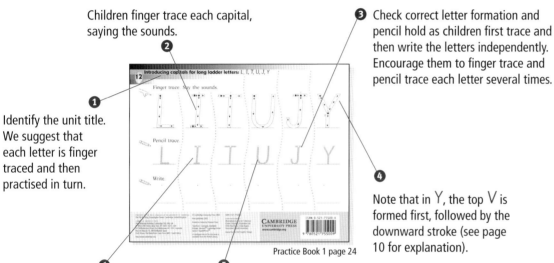

Practice Book 1 page 24

❹ Note that in Y, the top V is formed first, followed by the downward stroke (see page 10 for explanation).

❻ Can the children think of names that begin with all these letters? (e.g. Leroy, Izzy, Tom, Una, Jamila, Yvonne)

❺ Remember that there is no downward stroke and flick on the U as there is in the lower case letter.

Common errors

- starting with horizontals rather than the vertical line
- curving the J the wrong way
- inconsistent letter size
- Y – not positioning the V to allow room for the stick

Out and about activity

Encourage children to find horizontal and vertical lines in the environment (e.g. in fences, walls, zebra crossings, drainpipes, gates, window frames).

Take away

Children find and cut out the capital letters L, I, T, U, J, Y from old newspapers or magazines.

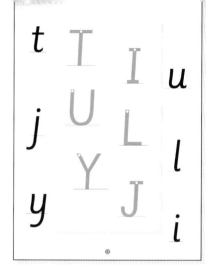

Big Book page 13

Introduce the page

- Encourage the children to talk about the page before you begin.
- Identify the fact that it is a matching game. Talk about the letter shapes and phonemes.
- Talk about when you would use capital letters (beginnings of sentences, names).

Demonstrate the letter formations

- Talk about the fact that all these letters are different in their lower case and capital forms.
- Talk about how many pencil strokes it takes to make each letter:
  1: U, L   2: T, J, Y   3: I
- U and J are the odd ones out as they each have a curve at the bottom: J curves to the left and U to the right.
  Show Me Children practise each capital letter in turn.
  Get Up and Go Ask the children to match the capitals to the lower case letters by drawing a line between the two.

CD-ROM

Unit focus: introducing the curly caterpillar letter family.
Phonic link: hearing initial phoneme **c**; alliteration in *curly caterpillar*.

Letter animation

Talk about the curly caterpillar family mnemonic. Play the letter animation and say the patter. Children make the letter shape and say the patter.

Sky writing

Children copy the three patterns which emphasise movements in the curly caterpillar family. Say "Make a curve." as children begin each movement.

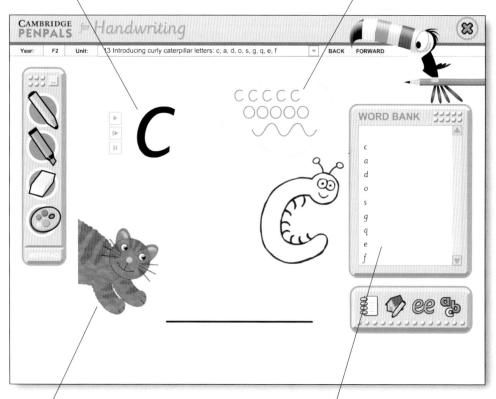

Challenge artwork

The picture illustrates a word beginning with the target letter. Children identify the picture word (cat). Write the word and establish the target letter.

Word bank

Choose a letter to discuss. Click on the letter to make it grey. Model and discuss the movements needed to form the letter.

Gross motor skills

- Children roll hoops to encourage a forward propelling action.
- Children join hands to form a large circle. Ask them to practise dancing clockwise and anticlockwise to become familiar with the difference – and to stop them getting dizzy!

Fine motor skills

- Children make long Plasticine sausages and then shape them into Os and Cs.
- Spread out large sheets of paper on the floor. Children make patterns with circles. Encourage them to try using different media.

Play and practise

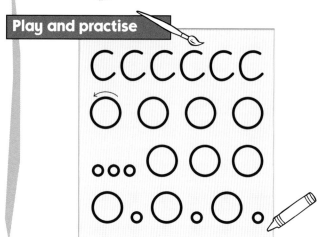

Practice Book warm up

🖐 Children sky write curly caterpillar patterns.

Independent work

① Identify the unit title.

② Children finger trace these letters saying the sound. Remind the children of the oral patter.

⑤ Can the children identify the pictures and the initial phoneme? Can they spot the extra c in *clock*? Children read the words and then trace the Cs.

⑥ Children write the missing Cs in the spaces. Can they think of another word beginning with C?

Introducing curly caterpillar letters: c, a, d, o, s, g, q, e, f

Finger trace. Say the sound.

c c c

Read and write.

at / at   clo k / lo k

Pencil trace.

Write.

Trace the patterns.

⑧ Children trace over the patterns.

Practice Book 2 pages 2–3

③ Check pencil holds while children pencil trace over the letters.

④ Check correct letter formation as children write the letter independently.

⑦ Children write a line of Cs. Check for pencil hold and correct letter formation.

Common errors

- starting at 12 o'clock rather than 1 o'clock
- finishing too close to the starting point on c
- breaking pencil flow and interrupting fluidity of movement

Out and about activity

Children look out for circles in the environment (e.g. wheels, windows, manhole covers). They could also search for caterpillars if it's the right time of year.

Take away

Children use **PCM 5 or 6** as curly caterpillar family pattern or letter practice.

Big Book page 14

Introduce the page

- Encourage the children to talk about the page before you begin.
- Point out the curly caterpillar artwork.

Skywriting patterns

- Emphasise the anticlockwise movement.

Demonstrate the letter formations

- Demonstrate the curly caterpillar pattern using the caterpillar picture and the oral letter family patter (see page 11).
- Emphasise the starting point and anticlockwise direction using the patter. If possible, refer to a clock to show the direction.
- Demonstrate the rest of the letters.
  Get Up and Go Ask the children to point to the starting point of each letter in the family.
- Invite the children to make sets with the letters. Some letters are short (c, o, e, a, s), some have an ascender (d), some have a descender (g, q) and f has both an ascender and a descender. Note which letters have an exit flick (a, d, q).
- Note that s and f are the odd ones out as the curly caterpillar is much smaller in these letters and sits in the top half.
- Point out that d doesn't begin at the top and goes up beyond its starting point.
  Show Me Children practise the letter c.

CD-ROM

Unit focus: introducing _d_ as a letter with an ascender and _a_ as a short letter.
Phonic links: hearing initial phoneme **d**; building CVC words.

Letter animations
Choose a letter. Play the letter animation and say the patter. Children make the letter shape and say the patter.

Sky writing
Children copy the three patterns which emphasise movements in the curly caterpillar family. Identify curves and straight lines in curly caterpillar letters.

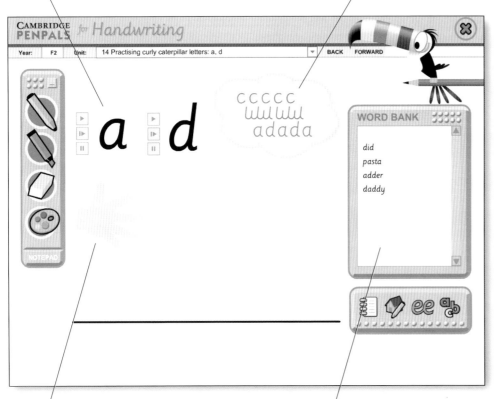

Challenge artwork
The picture illustrates a word that features both target letters. Children identify the picture word (hand). Write the word and establish the target letters.

Word bank
Choose a word to discuss. Click on the word to make the target graphemes grey. Model and discuss the letter formation and phonemes.

Gross motor skills
- Children try writing _as_ and _ds_ as if their nose were a pencil.
- Children use ribbons or streamers to make anticlockwise circles in the air.

Fine motor skills
- Children thread beads or pasta tubes onto a string to make a necklace.
- Children use tweezers to pick up sequins or buttons and place them onto outline shapes of _as_ and _ds_.

Play and practise

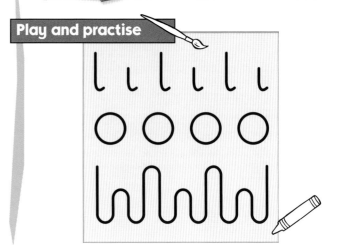

Practice Book warm up

Practise the difference between a and d in the air. Children sky write the letter a, and when you say "Up!", they sky write a d instead.

Independent work

① Identify the unit title.

② Children finger trace these letters, saying the sounds.

③ Remind the children about the tall d and the short a.

⑥ Can the children identify the pictures, and the phoneme at the end of the words *sad* and *lad*? Children read the words and then trace the letters.

⑦ Children write the missing letters in the spaces.

⑨ Children trace over the patterns and give the sad lad some hair.

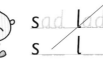

Practice Book 2 pages 4–5

④ Check pencil holds while children pencil trace over the letters.

⑤ Check correct letter formation as children write the letters independently. Make sure they start at the caterpillar's head.

⑧ Children write a line of ads. Check for pencil hold and correct letter formation.

Common errors

- starting too far to the right
- ball and stick formation
- not going high enough with the d ascender and then adding it afterwards
- not completing the circle before making the upward stroke
- starting the d at the top

Out and about activity

Chalk giant as and ds on the playground for children to run round. Check that they are running up the stick and back down again, ending with a flick.

Take away

Children practise writing *dad* and *daddy*.

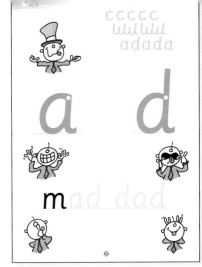

Big Book page 15

Introduce the page

- Encourage the children to talk about the page before you begin.
- Talk about the pictures and the initial phoneme **d**, the **ad** rime and the high-frequency word *dad*.

Skywriting patterns

- Emphasise the anticlockwise direction and whizzing up high.

Demonstrate the letter formations

Get Up and Go Children identify the curly caterpillar in a and d.

- Trace over the a and the d, talking about the letter formation.
- Talk about the height of the letter d.
- Both letters sit on the line and have an exit flick.
  Show Me Children practise each letter in turn.
- Trace over the as and ds in the phrase.
- Can the children think of another word that rhymes with *dad* and *mad*? (e.g. *sad, bad*)

CD-ROM

Unit focus: introducing o and s together as short letters, stressing the anticlockwise direction.
Phonic link: hearing initial phoneme **s**.

Letter animations
Choose a letter. Play the letter animation and say the patter. Children make the letter shape and say the patter.

Sky writing
Children copy the three patterns which emphasise movements in the curly caterpillar family. Identify curves in different directions in curly caterpillar letters.

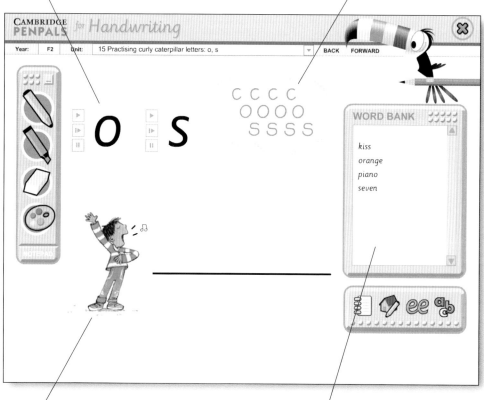

Challenge artwork
The picture illustrates words that feature both target letters. Children identify the picture words (sing a song). Write the words and establish the target letters.

Word bank
Choose a word to discuss. Click on the word to make the target graphemes grey. Model and discuss the letter formation and phonemes.

Gross motor skills
- Children jump in and out of hoops.
- Draw clocks with chalk on the playground. Children run round them, first clockwise and then anticlockwise, starting and finishing at different numbers.
- Draw joined c patterns (like waves) in chalk on the playground for children to run round. Use language like *go up, back and round, then whoosh … up again!*

Fine motor skills
- Using cotton buds, children make circular patterns of dots.
- Children draw circles in sand.
- Children make s and o patterns within outlines like this:

Play and practise

Practice Book warm up

✋ Children practise the anticlockwise direction. They could sing *Round And Round The Garden* (see **Foundation 1 CD, track 22; Teacher's Book, page 46**) while making anticlockwise circles on the palms of their hands.

Independent work

1 Identify the unit title.

2 Children finger trace these letters, saying the sounds.

3 Remind the children that the s curves back on itself.

6 Can the children identify the pictures and the initial phoneme? If they are ready, introduce the alliterative word *stripy*. At this point (or later in the session) they can make all the socks stripy.

7 Children find the letters s and o and trace over them.

Practice Book 2 pages 6–7

10 Children trace over the patterns.

4 Check pencil holds while children pencil trace over the letters.

5 Check correct letter formation as children write the letters independently.

8 Children write the missing letters in the spaces.

9 Children write a line of os and ss. Check for pencil hold and correct letter formation.

Common errors

- not starting at 1 o'clock
- crossing the o
- not closing the o

- contortions of s – especially making it too big
- reversal of s

Take away

Children draw round different coins to make o patterns. They should always draw the circles anticlockwise.

Out and about activity

Ask children to find os and ss on signs around the school.

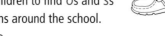

Big Book page 16

Introduce the page

- Encourage the children to talk about the page before you begin.
- Talk about the picture and the initial phoneme **s**. Invite the children to make another phrase with words that begin with s or o (e.g. *six orange socks*).

Skywriting patterns

- Emphasise the anticlockwise direction. Have fun with the flow of the second pattern.

Demonstrate the letter formations

- Trace over the o and the s, talking about the letter formation.
- Both letters sit on the line and are short but neither has an exit flick.
- Point out that s comes back on itself. Remind the children where the curly caterpillar is in s (sitting in the top half) and that it is smaller than in the other curly caterpillar letters.
- Point out that o and s are the same size.
  Show Me Children practise each letter in turn.
  Get Up and Go Ask the children to point to the ss and o in the phrase *silly old sausages*.
- Trace over the letters s and o in the phrase.

CD-ROM

Unit focus: introducing g and q together as letters with descenders (one curved and one with a flick) and stressing the anticlockwise direction.

Phonic link: hearing initial phonemes **g** and **q**.

Gross motor skills

- Children perform contrasting movements to music (e.g. slow/fast, soft and gentle/hard and spiky).
- Children use ribbons, streamers or frisbees (or paper plates) to practise wrist flick movements.

Fine motor skills

- Prepare a laminated A4 card with the curly caterpillar shapes drawn on it in marker pen. Children roll out Plasticine and model the shapes by placing the Plasticine on top.

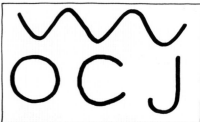

Letter animations

Choose a letter. Play the letter animation and say the patter. Children make the letter shape and say the patter.

Sky writing

Children copy the three patterns which emphasise movements in the curly caterpillar family. Identify curves in different directions and straight lines in curly caterpillar letters.

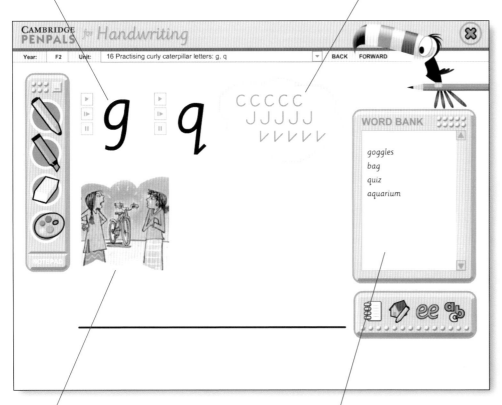

Play and practise

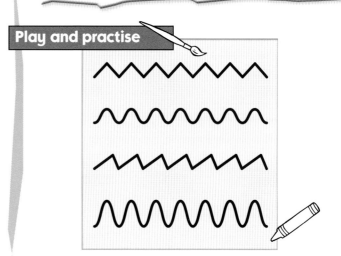

Challenge artwork

The picture illustrates words that feature both target letters. Children identify the picture words (quarrelling girls). Write the words and establish the target letters.

Word bank

Choose a word to discuss. Click on the word to make the target graphemes grey. Model and discuss the letter formation and phonemes.

Big Book page 17

Practice Book warm up

- 🖐 Children make their hands move in soft waves in all directions.
- 🖐 Children make their hands move in zig-zags in all directions.

Independent work

① Identify the unit title. You can choose to work across the page dealing with g and q together or you can work through g and then q.

② Children finger trace these letters, saying the sounds.

③ Check pencil holds while children pencil trace over the letters. Remind them about the descenders. The g has a curved descender that goes to the left (like y and j) and the q has a flick descender that goes to the right.

⑤ Can the children identify the picture?

⑥ Read the phrase together. Children find the letters g and q and trace over them.

⑨ Children trace over the patterns.

Practice Book 2 pages 8–9

④ Check correct letter formation as children write the letters independently.

⑦ Children write the missing gs and q in the spaces.

⑧ Children write a line of gs and then qs. Check for pencil hold and correct letter formation. Talk about these letters both having a descender.

Common errors

- incorrect length of descender
- the flick of q to the left
- directionality of both letters

Take away

Children fill a hollow g with gs and a hollow q with qs.

Out and about activity

Ask children to look out for soft curves and sharp flicks in trees (e.g. *curves*: flowers, leaves, crown of tree; *flicks*: branches, stems).

Introduce the page

- Encourage the children to talk about the page before you begin. Discuss the patterns in the pictures.
- Talk about the picture and the initial phonemes **g** and **q**.
- Invite the children to change the q word for another one that begins with q (e.g. *quietly*). Note that q is always followed by u. Now ask the children to think of an alternative g word (e.g. *gallop*).

Skywriting patterns

- Emphasise the anticlockwise direction. Have fun with the curve and the flick.

Demonstrate the letter formations

- Trace over the g and the q, talking about the letter formation.
- Both letters sit on the line and have descenders. The descender on the g is curved and goes to the left. The descender on the q is a flick and goes to the right.
  Show Me Children practise each letter in turn.
  Get Up and Go Ask the children to point to the g and the q in the sentence *Now go quickly!*
- Trace over the g and the q in the sentence.

Unit focus: introducing f as a tall letter with a descender in relation to e as a short letter.
Phonic link: hearing initial phonemes **e** and **f**.

Gross motor skills

- Children use ribbons or streamers to make vertical snake patterns.
- Children use skipping ropes to make snakes on the floor. They can make their snakes wriggle by moving one end of the rope.
- Children try skipping with a rope.

Fine motor skills

- Provide long strips of paper with long wiggly lines for cutting practice.
- Children finger paint fish or snakes and decorate them with curly patterns.

Letter animations
Choose a letter. Play the letter animation and say the patter. Children make the letter shape and say the patter.

Sky writing
Children copy the three patterns which emphasise movements in the curly caterpillar family. Identify curves in different directions and straight lines in curly caterpillar letters.

Play and practise

Challenge artwork
The picture illustrates a word that features both target letters. Children identify the picture word (faces). Write the word and establish the target letters.

Word bank
Choose a word to discuss. Click on the word to make the target graphemes grey. Model and discuss the letter formation and phonemes.

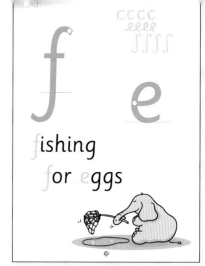

Big Book page 18

Practice Book warm up

✋ Children practise the skywriting patterns.

Independent work

❶ Identify the unit title. You can choose to work across the page dealing with e and f together or you can work through e and then f.

❷ Children finger trace these letters, saying the sounds.

❸ Check pencil holds while children pencil trace over the letters. Remind the children about the starting point of the e.

❻ Can the children identify the picture?

❼ Read the phrase together. Children find the letters e and f and trace over them.

Practice Book 2 pages 10–11

❿ Children trace over the patterns.

❾ Children write a line of es and fs. Check for pencil hold and correct letter formation. Talk about e being a short letter and f a tall letter with a descender.

❹ Check correct letter formation as children write the letters independently.

❺ Note that f is a tall letter: its top point is higher than the top of other letters with descenders (like g, j, p, q and y).

❽ Children write the missing es and f in the spaces.

Common errors

- reversing the e
- exaggerating the f descender and/or the cross bar
- making f too like s

Take away

Children fill a fish shape with es and fs.

Out and about activity

Children look for es and fs in notices around the school.

Introduce the page

- Encourage the children to talk about the page.
- Talk about the picture and the initial phonemes **e** and **f**.
- Ask the children: which sound does *elephant* begin with?

Skywriting patterns

- Emphasise the anticlockwise movements of the patterns. Enjoy the change from horizontal to vertical – spiral across and then down, or down and then across.

Demonstrate the letter formations

- Trace over e and f and talk about letter formation.
- Point out that e starts with a left-to-right line before it goes into the curly caterpillar shape.
- f begins like a curly caterpillar and then has a long descender that curves to the left like the descender of a g. It then has a cross bar that goes from left to right. It has an ascender and a descender.
  Get Up and Go Ask the children to point to the e and fs in the phrase *fishing for eggs*.
- Trace over the e and fs in the phrase.
  Show Me Children practise each letter in turn.
- Point out the ss and talk about how they are different from the fs (s is a short letter that sits on the line; f has both an ascender and a descender).

CD-ROM

Unit focus: revisiting all the curly caterpillar letters in context.
Phonic link: recognising all the letters in the curly caterpillar family as letters and phonemes.

Letter animations
Choose a letter. Play the letter animation and say the patter. Children make the letter shape and say the patter.

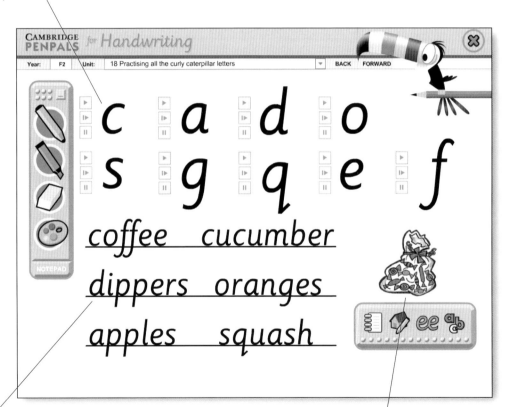

Words
Click on a word to make the target graphemes grey. Model and discuss the letter formation and phonemes.

Challenge artwork
The picture illustrates words featuring some of the target letters. Children identify the picture words (bag of sweets). Write the words and establish the target letters.

Gross motor skills
- Children use ribbons or streamers to practise all the curly caterpillar letters.
- Children lie on a mat and make curled shapes with their bodies. They should twist, turn and curl into lots of different shapes.
- Children join hands to make a big circle and dance round, first clockwise and then anticlockwise.

Fine motor skills
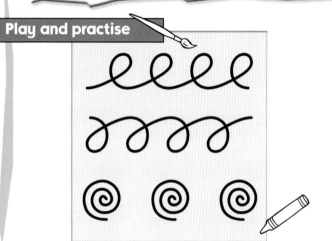
- Children fill in a flower outline, writing a different curly caterpillar letter, and using a different writing tool and colour in each section.
- Children make play dough cookies, kneading, prodding, rolling and bashing the dough. They can cut out the middles to make 'Polo' cookies!

Play and practise

The fluffy grey
cat was quick ...

but the dormouse
was quicker!

Big Book page 19

Children practise making a c and an o using the thumb and index finger of their left hand. Repeat using each of the fingers in turn. They then make os using the right hand.

Independent work

1 Identify the unit title.

2 Children pencil trace the first letter of each line and then complete the line independently. Revise the oral patter if necessary.

4 Remind the children about short letters and letters with ascenders and descenders. Remind them about the flick descender of q and the uniqueness of f.

Practice Book 2 pages 12–13

3 Check correct letter formation and pencil hold as children write the letters independently.

5 Children trace over the snails' shells, starting in the middle.

6 If time, children may like to decorate the caterpillar with patterns of letters from this family. Encourage pattern-making rather than simple colouring.

Introduce the page

- Begin by recapping the letters in the curly caterpillar family (c, a, d, o, s, g, q, e, f).
- Encourage the children to talk about the page before you begin.
- Talk about the picture and read the words.
  Get Up and Go Ask the children to find the examples of each letter in the sentence.
- Remind the children of the correct formation as you trace over the letters.
  Show Me Children practise each letter in turn.

Common errors

- reversing letters
- starting at 12 o'clock instead of 1 o'clock
- leaving gaps in the letter
- descenders too long/ascenders too high
- using unnecessary pencil lifts in letter formation

Out and about activity

Look at print in the classroom. Ask the children to search for curly caterpillar letters. They can make a simple chart and tick each time they see one.

Take away

Children can use (or re-use) **PCM 6** according to their individual practice needs.

 **CD-ROM**

Unit focus: introducing the zig-zag monster letter family.
Phonic link: hearing the repetition of the initial phoneme **z** in *zig-zag*.

Letter animation
Talk about the zig-zag monster family mnemonic. Play the letter animation and say the patter. Children make the letter shape and say the patter.

Sky writing
Children copy the three patterns which emphasise movements in the zig-zag monster family. Identify straight and sloping lines.

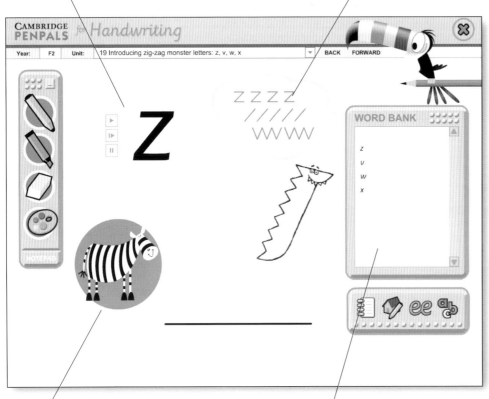

Challenge artwork
The picture illustrates a word beginning with the target letter. Children identify the picture word (zebra). Write the word and establish the target letter.

Word bank
Choose a letter to discuss. Click on the letter to make it grey. Model and discuss the movements needed to form the letter.

Gross motor skills
- Children use stilts (the type that look like upside-down flowerpots) to develop balance and arm muscles.
- Children run, walk, hop and jump along diagonal lines chalked on the floor.
- Make benches into a zig-zag pathway for children to balance along.

Fine motor skills
- Draw zig-zag lines on pages of textured paper from wallpaper books. Invite children to cut these out and then enjoy feeling the zig-zag shape. They may like to do some rubbings too.
- Children make zig-zag patterns with pipe cleaners.

Play and practise

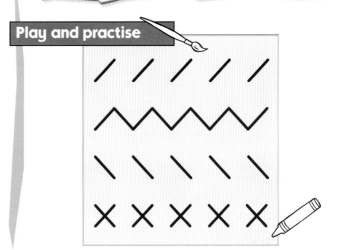

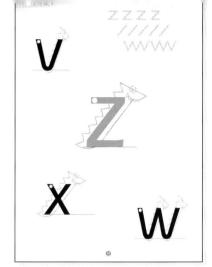

Practice Book warm up

🖐 Children practise sky writing zig-zag patterns.

Independent work

① Identify the unit title.

② Children finger trace these letters, saying the sound. Remind the children to use the oral patter.

⑤ Can the children identify the picture and the initial **z** phonemes? Read the words and then trace the Zs. If time, children make zig-zag patterns on the zip.

⑥ Children write the missing Zs in the spaces.

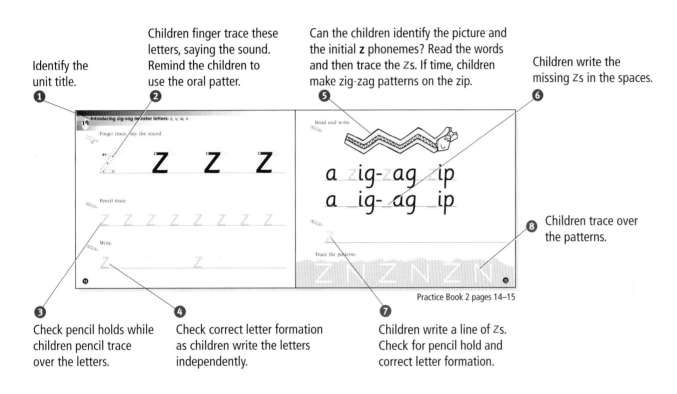

Practice Book 2 pages 14–15

⑧ Children trace over the patterns.

③ Check pencil holds while children pencil trace over the letters.

④ Check correct letter formation as children write the letters independently.

⑦ Children write a line of Zs. Check for pencil hold and correct letter formation.

Common errors

- misjudging the angles so the two zig-zags are uneven
- reversing the direction of movements
- not using a horizontal line at the top and bottom

Take away

Children use **PCM 7 or 8** as zig-zag family pattern or letter practice.

Out and about activity

Go for a walk and ask children to look for diagonal lines (e.g. fences, road markings, scaffolding). Children record the lines and patterns they see.

Introduce the page

- Encourage the children to talk about the page before you begin.
- Identify the zig-zag monster artwork.
  Show Me Can the children draw a zig-zag monster?

Skywriting patterns

- Emphasise the diagonal lines. You may prefer to call them 'sloping' lines.

Demonstrate the letter formations

- Demonstrate the zig-zag pattern using the monster picture and the oral letter family patter (see page 11). Emphasise the starting point and use the patter. Can the children see the diagonal line in each letter?
  Get Up and Go Ask the children to point to the starting point of each letter in the family.
- Demonstrate the rest of the letters.
- Note that V and W are very similar – W has two monsters instead of one.
- X is formed by writing left to right and then right to left to make a criss-cross monster.
- Z goes left to right, then backwards and then left to right again.
  Show Me Children practise the letter Z.

CD-ROM

Unit focus: introducing v, w and x together as short letters and stressing the diagonal lines.
Phonic link: hearing initial phonemes **v** and **w** and spotting **x** (**ks**) as a final sound in a CVC word.

Gross motor skills
- Children throw beanbags or balls overarm to encourage spatial awareness and to develop a sense of upper arm force (away from the body).
- Children make zig-zag letters with partners using their whole bodies.

Fine motor skills
- Using finger paints, children make zig-zag patterns using their fingers, cotton buds, small combs or plastic forks.
- Children make Plasticine snakes and then model them into zig-zag patterns.
- Children add teeth to a crocodile.

Letter animations
Choose a letter. Play the letter animation and say the patter. Children make the letter shape and say the patter.

Sky writing
Children copy the three patterns which emphasise movements in the zig-zag monster family. Identify straight and sloping lines in zig-zag monster letters.

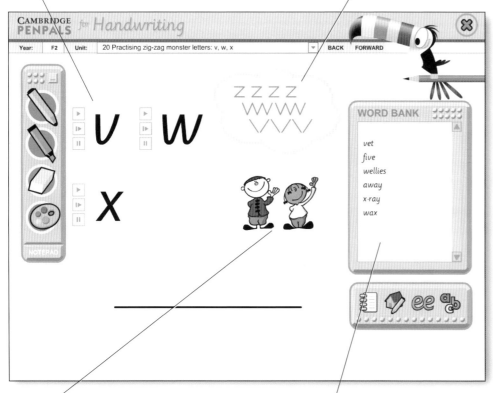

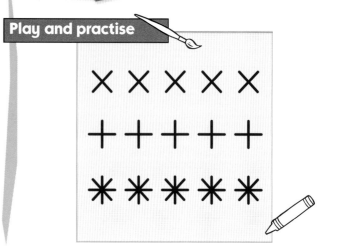

Play and practise

Challenge artwork
The picture illustrates a word that features two of the target letters. Children identify the picture word (wave). Write the word and establish the target letters.

Word bank
Choose a word to discuss. Click on the word to make the target graphemes grey. Model and discuss the letter formation and phonemes.

Practice Book warm up

- Children pretend to make their arms blow in the wind and then make their arms and fingers rain.
- Children make one finger on each hand into a + and then rotate to a x.

Independent work

1 Identify the unit title. You can choose to work across the page dealing with v, w and x together or you can work through them one after another.

2 Children finger trace these letters saying the sounds.

5 Check the left-to-right and then right-to-left formation of x very carefully.

6 Can the children identify the picture?

7 Read the phrase together. Children find the letters v, w and x and trace over them.

9 Children write a line of vs, ws and xs. Check for pencil hold and correct letter formation.

10 Children trace over the patterns.

Practice Book 2 pages 16–17

3 Check pencil holds while children pencil trace over the letters. Remind the children that these are all short letters but they all have a zig-zag or crossing-over of lines in them. You may want to talk about diagonal lines if this is appropriate to your class.

4 Check correct letter formation as children write the letters independently.

8 Children write the missing v, w and x in the spaces.

Common errors

- w too wide or too tall
- incorrect formation of x
- starting at the bottom of x

Take away

Children can use (or re-use) **PCM 8** according to their individual practice needs.

Out and about activity

Children plant seeds or place pebbles or stones in zig-zag patterns.

Introduce the page

- Encourage the children to talk about the page before you begin.
- Talk about the picture, the initial phonemes **w** and **v** and the **x** sound at the end of *box*.

Skywriting patterns

- Emphasise the initial downward stroke on the first pattern. Then enjoy making crosses in the air.

Demonstrate the letter formations

- Trace over the letters, emphasising the formation.
- All these letters sit on the line and are short. None has an exit flick.
- Remember that w is like two vs.
- x begins with a left-to-right action followed by a break and then a right-to-left stroke.
  Show Me Children practise each letter in turn.
  Get Up and Go Ask the children to point to the v, w and x in the phrase.
- Trace over the ws, v and x in the phrase.

CD-ROM

Unit focus: introducing capitals for letters in the curly caterpillar family.
Phonic links: recognising phonemes associated with capital and lower case letters c, a, d, o, s, g, q, e and f; ensuring that children understand that capital and lower case letters represent the same phonemes.

Letter animations

Choose a letter. Play the letter animation and say the patter.
Children make the letter shape and say the patter. Ask
children to show the lower case equivalent of the letter.

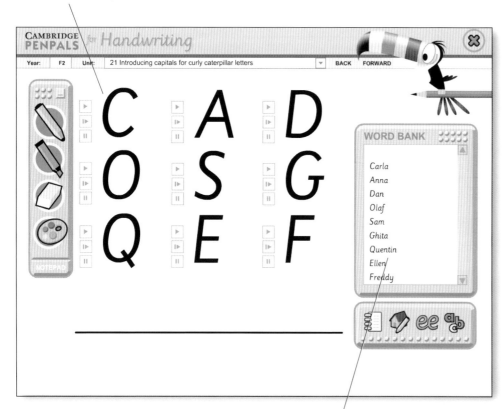

Word bank

Choose a name to discuss. Click on the name to
make the capital letter grey. Model and discuss
the movements needed to form the letter.

Gross motor skills

- Children roll hoops in the playground or the hall to encourage a forward propelling action.
- Children make arches with their arms for others to skip through.
- Children use ribbons or streamers to make anticlockwise circles in the air.

Fine motor skills

- Prepare a laminated A4 card with the capital letters drawn on it in marker pen. Children roll out Plasticine and model the letters by placing the Plasticine on top.

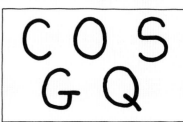

Play and practise

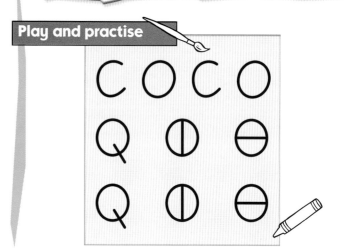

Practice Book warm up

✋ Children practise making anticlockwise arm movements.

Independent work

Identify the unit title. We suggest that each letter is finger traced and then practised in turn.

1

Children finger trace each capital saying the sounds.

2

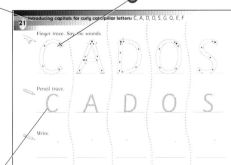
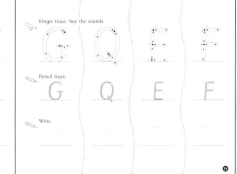

Practice Book 2 pages 18–19

3

Check correct letter formation and pencil hold as children first trace and then write the letters independently. Encourage them to finger trace and pencil trace each letter several times.

4

Can the children think of names that begin with these letters? (e.g. Darren, Clyde, Oliver, Quentin, Ellen, Sanjit, George, Ahmed, Fiona)

Common errors

- writing G and Q like lower case g and q (like other letters in this family)

- not joining the head to the tail on O and Q

- imbalance of the curve sizes in S, or exaggeration of the backward swing

- beginning letters at 12 o'clock not 1 o'clock

- incorrect placement of the line across Q

Out and about activity

Children play noughts and crosses outside using chalk.

Take away

Children find two signs written in capitals and copy them.

Introduce the page

- Encourage the children to talk about the page.
- Identify the fact that it is a matching game that they have met before. Talk about the letter shapes and phonemes.
- Again, talk about when you would use capital letters (beginnings of sentences, names).

Demonstrate the letter formations

- Trace over the letters, discussing the formations.
- Talk about the fact that three of these letters (C, O and S) are the same in lower case and capital form. The capitals are simply bigger.
- Talk about how many pencil strokes it takes to make each letter.
  1: C, S, O 2: Q, G, D 3: A, F 4: E
- Talk about O and Q being the same apart from the line in Q.
- Talk about G and the short cross bar.
  Show Me Children practise each letter in turn.
  Get Up and Go Ask the children to match the capitals to the lower case letters by drawing a line between the two.

CD-ROM

Unit focus: introducing capitals for letters in the zig-zag monster letter family.

Phonic link: recognising phonemes associated with capital and lower case letters z, v, w and x; ensuring that children understand that capital and lower case letters represent the same phonemes. You may want to remind the children that x makes a **ks** sound in a word and a **z** sound at the beginning of a word.

Letter animations

Choose a letter. Play the letter animation and say the patter. Children make the letter shape and say the patter. Ask children to show the lower case equivalent of the letter.

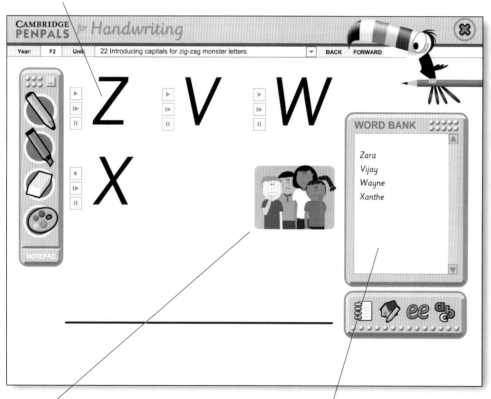

Challenge artwork

The picture features a group of children with names beginning with the target letter. Children guess the names. Write the names and establish the target letter.

Word bank

Choose a name to discuss. Click on the name to make the capital letter grey. Model and discuss the movements needed to form the letter.

Gross motor skills

- Make benches into a zig-zag pathway for children to travel along.
- Chalk some large squares onto the playground and draw in the diagonal lines. Label each corner with a zig-zag letter. Working in pairs, children give each other instructions to move to another letter, but they must always travel along a diagonal line.

Fine motor skills

- Children use finger paints to make patterns with / and \ lines.
- Children draw letters on each other's backs and try to guess which letter it is.

Play and practise

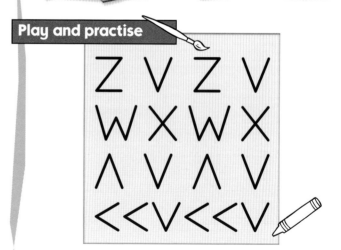

Big Book page 23

Practice Book warm up

🖐 Children make zig-zags in the air using their hands, index fingers, heads …

🖐 Children practise crossing each finger with the thumb on each hand. Children shake their fingers out at the end.

Independent work

Identify the unit title. We suggest that each letter is finger traced and then practised in turn.

1

Children finger trace each capital saying the sound and the oral letter family patter.

2

Look at these capitals in terms of pencil strokes:
1: W, V, Z
2: X

5

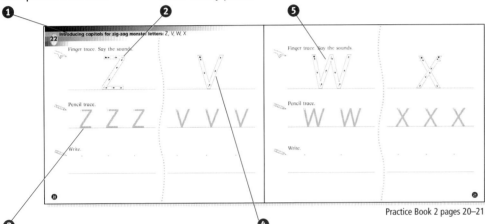

Practice Book 2 pages 20–21

3

Check correct letter formation and pencil hold as children first trace and then write the letters independently. Encourage them to finger trace and pencil trace each letter several times.

4

V, W, X and Z are the same as their lower case forms.

6

Can the children think of names that begin with these letters? (e.g. Zak, Veena, Wesley, Xavier)

Common errors

● X – written as + or with misjudged angles

● Z – reversal of Z and/or confusion with S

● W – middle point being too high

Out and about activity

Ask children to find words around the school or classroom that have zig-zag capital letters in them (e.g. FIRE EXIT, WELCOME, CLASS FIVE).

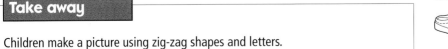

Take away

Children make a picture using zig-zag shapes and letters.

Introduce the page

● Encourage the children to talk about the page before you begin.

● Identify the fact that it is a matching game that they have met before. Talk about the letter shapes and phonemes.

● Again, talk about when you would use capital letters (beginnings of sentences, names).

Demonstrate the letter formations

● Talk about the fact that v, w, x, and z are the same in lower case and capital form – the capital is just bigger.

● Talk about how many pencil strokes it takes to make each letter:
1: W, V, Z   2: X

● Trace each letter in turn.
Show Me Children practise each letter in turn.
Get Up and Go Ask the children to match the capitals to the lower case letters by drawing a line between the two.

CD-ROM

Unit focus: introducing *ch*, *th* and *sh* together as common digraphs. (NB: these digraphs provide an opportunity to introduce the notion of joining – in each case, the two letters make one sound and they can be written together too.)
Phonic link: phonemes **ch**, **th** and **sh**.

Letter animations

For each grapheme, talk about which family each letter comes from. Choose a grapheme. Play the animation and say the patter. Children make the letter shapes individually before combining them.

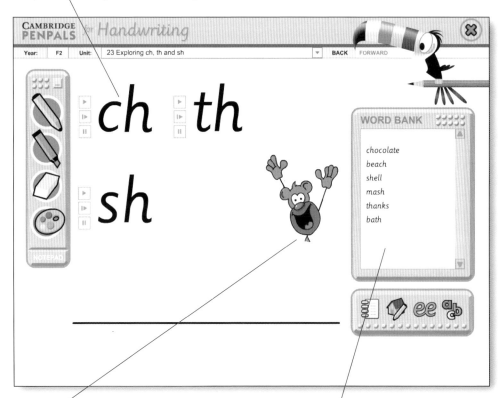

Challenge artwork

The picture illustrates words that feature one pair of the target letters. Children identify the picture words (cheering chimp). Write the words and establish the target letters.

Word bank

Choose a word to discuss. Click on the word to make the target graphemes grey. Model and discuss the letter formation and phonemes.

Gross motor skills

- Working in the hall, give children pairs of instructions to demonstrate the idea of linking two actions, for example, 'Walk along the beam and then jump on to the mat,' or, 'Run at the ropes and swing.'
- Make and distribute labels – *c*, *h* or *s*. (Note that you will need twice the number of *h* labels to ensure that all the *c* and *s* children can find a partner.) Children run around and when the whistle blows they have to find a partner to make a *ch*, *th* or *sh*. Can they tell you what sound they make together?

Fine motor skills

- Using salt or sand on a tray, children make flowing patterns.
- Children thread beads onto a string that is knotted at the bottom.
- Children try sewing cards with bodkin needles.

Take away

Children experiment with 'flowing' or joined patterns on long strips of paper.

Out and about activity

Children make posters for the school using the *ch*, *th* and *sh* digraphs, for example *No shouting! No chatting! Lots of thinking!*

ch   sh
th

children ...

chatting

shouting

thinking

Big Book page 24

Practice Book warm up

Children pretend to rock a baby in their arms.

Independent work

Identify the unit title. You can choose to work across the pages or you can work through them consecutively.

1

Children finger trace the letters, saying the sounds.

2

Check pencil holds while children pencil trace over the letters. Remind the children that the **ch** sound is made by a short letter, c, followed by a tall letter, h. The **th** sound is made by a tall letter, t, followed by another tall letter, h. Point out that the t is a little bit shorter than the h. The **sh** sound is made by a short letter, s, followed by a tall letter, h.

3

Can the children identify the pictures?

6

Read the sentences together. Children find the digraphs ch, th and sh and trace over them. Point out the capital letter at the beginning of the sentences.

7

Practice Book 2 pages 22–23

Practice Book 2 page 24

"Cheep, cheep," said the chicks.

Shsh, sheep sleeping!

4 Check correct letter formation as children write the letters independently.

5 As ch, th and sh are important digraphs that children will be meeting in their early phonic work, you may want to use them as examples of joining. The letters join together to make one sound – **ch**, **th** or **sh**. Explain that these can be written in a joined way (show ch, th or sh joined). We have provided a simple practice line at the bottom of the page for those who wish to use it.

8 Children write a line of chs and ths. Check for pencil hold and correct letter formation. If you are happy for the children to practise these in a joined style, encourage them to do so.

9 Children trace over the patterns.

Introduce the page

- Encourage the children to talk about the page before you begin.
- Talk about the pictures and the initial phonemes.

Skywriting patterns

- Emphasise the flow of the movement.

Demonstrate the letter formations

- Revisit the formation of both letters in each of the digraphs.
- Highlight the fact that t is shorter than h.
  Show Me Children practise each digraph in turn.
  Get Up and Go Ask the children to point to the digraphs in the phrase.
- Trace over the chs, th and sh in the phrase.
- Ask the children: can you think of some other things that these children might be doing that begin with these digraphs? (e.g. chilling, cheating, shooing, shushing, thanking, thumping)

Common errors

- t and h being the same size (t should be shorter)

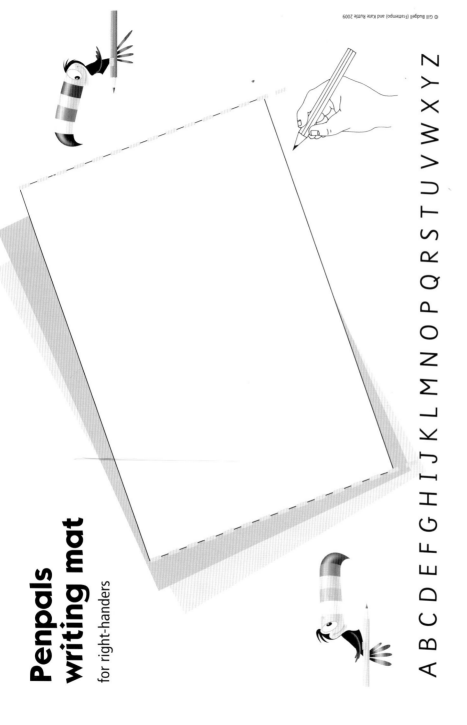

a b c d e f g h i j k l m n o p q r s t u v w x y z

Penpals
writing mat
for right-handers

A B C D E F G H I J K L M N O P Q R S T U V W X Y Z

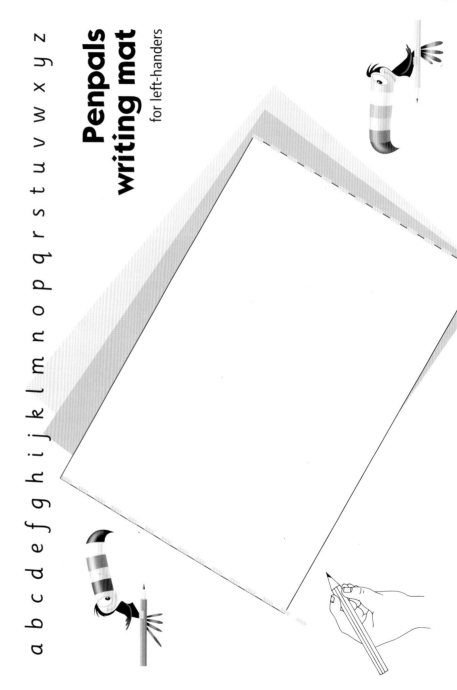

a b c d e f g h i j k l m n o p q r s t u v w x y z

Penpals
writing mat
for left-handers

A B C D E F G H I J K L M N O P Q R S T U V W X Y Z

Name

Date

Copy the patterns.

1

Name

Date

Trace and write the letters.

Talk about the tails of these letters.

2

UNIT 6 — Pattern practice

Name

Date

Copy the patterns.

l l l

r r

m m

h m

4

UNIT 6 — Letter practice

Name

Date

Trace and write the letters.

Talk about the difference between these letters.

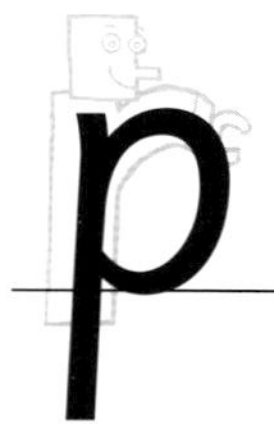

r

h

b

p

m

n

p

k

Name  Date

Copy the patterns.

OO

oOo

CCC

eee

Penpals for Handwriting: Foundation 2 **Introducing curly caterpillar letters**

Name  Date

Trace and write the letters.

c   a   d

o   d   e

f   q   g

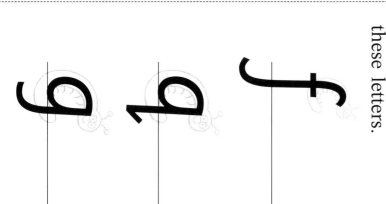

Talk about the tails of these letters.

Penpals for Handwriting: Foundation 2 **Introducing curly caterpillar letters**

UNIT 19 Pattern practice

Name

Date

Copy the patterns.

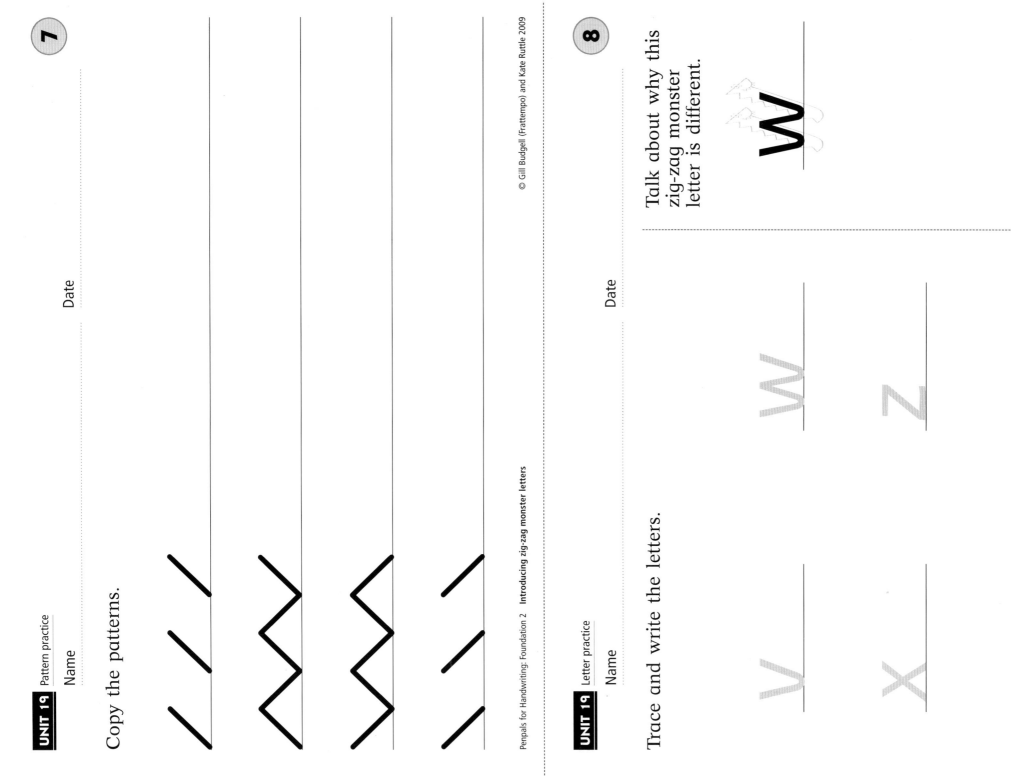

UNIT 19 Letter practice

Name

Date

Trace and write the letters.

Talk about why this zig-zag monster letter is different.